·A·N·
AFRICAN
EXPERIENCE

·AN· AFRICAN EXPERIENCE

WILDLIFE ART AND ADVENTURE IN KENYA

S·I·M·O·N · C·O·M·B·E·S

FOREWORD BY DAVID SHEPHERD

CLIVE HOLLOWAY BOOKS
LONDON

First published in Great Britain in 1989 by
Clive Holloway Books,
48 Baldry Gardens,
London SW16

British Library Cataloguing in Publication Data
Combes, Simon
    An African experience – wildlife art and adventure in
    Kenya.
    1. English paintings – Biographies
    I. Title
    759.2

    ISBN 1 85310 124 9

Designed by Nigel Partridge
Typeset by DP Photosetting, Aylesbury, Buckinghamshire
Colour separations by Columbia Offset, Singapore
Printed in West Germany by
Mohndruck Graphische Betriebe GmbH

FRONTISPIECE: TREE LION

Many theories have been given as to why the lions in Lake
Manyara Park so readily climb trees. Some say it is because the
particular acacias (*Acacia tortillis*) that grow there are so easy to
climb. Others suppose that the cats are either trying to escape
the swarms of flies, or catch a little cool breeze in that humid
climate. Whatever the reason, it is a unique spectacle, the tawny
bodies draped loose-limbed and relaxed along the dark, almost
black, branches.

Sometimes a herd of elephants will inadvertently approach a
lion-infested tree. The lions will be galvanised, springing to
alertness and scrambling to the ground with little skill or
dignity. I have never witnessed it, but imagine that a lion would
be in grave trouble if cornered up a tree by elephants.

I have great respect for the Manyara lions. During a recent visit
I watched with awe as a dawn drama unfolded. A great brute of
a lion ambushed a fully-grown buffalo on the lake shore. As the
lion clung to the buffalo's nose, its forepaws wrapped around its
horns, the bull swung his head from side to side, wiping the
lion all over the ground in a vain effort to dislodge its
tormentor. Finally, the buffalo fell to the ground with exhaustion
as the lion consolidated its suffocating hold over the muzzle. It
was a titanic struggle.

CONTENTS

To "The Fossils"

FOREWORD

All the artists I know are such super people, and Simon is certainly one of them. However, he does make me feel so very old when he says, in his very flattering and over-generous comments, that he thinks I to some degree inspired him to start painting wildlife! When I first went to Kenya to begin my career, he, as a very small boy, was getting upset about losing his favourite caterpillar! Anybody who gets upset about important issues like this must be a nice chap!

Without wishing to give too many secrets away about Simon's behaviour at parties, he also, on one particular occasion, has made me feel very young. Like every wildlife artist I know he feels he owes an enormous debt of gratitude to the wildlife that has brought him such success. That is why we always meet at fund raising parties, in America and elsewhere. It was after one such event in Connecticut, when we had jointly raised, with others, a large amount of money for the few remaining rhino in Kenya, that I realised what a multi-talented man Simon is – he could well have been in a circus! Admittedly it needs a few drinks to perform such activities, but to the enormous amusement of all of us going back to our hotel in our bus, I suddenly looked round and saw Simon swinging upside down from his arms on the luggage rack, his knees tucked in above his chest. Not to be outdone, I was determined, at an age almost old enough to be his father, to emulate him – indeed, outdo him. To my delight, I succeeded with, apparently, no adverse effect on my anatomy – not so far anyway! So perhaps I am not quite so old.

Simon's book is not only a treasure trove of paintings. It is a marvellous story of adventure which makes *Out of Africa* seem tame. I am particularly flattered and delighted to write this short foreword because, clearly, Simon's life has taken a path very similar to mine. We both have a great interest in and involvement with the fighting services. He remembers the early days in Kenya, when there was more game and fewer people. He writes about his life in an amusing, highly informative and thought-provoking way. Here is a man who uses his many talents not only to give enormous pleasure to a great many people, but also is fully aware, as I am, of the dangers which face wildlife and the environment from the world's most dangerous animal – man.

As I have already said, Simon flattered me in suggesting that I had some influence on his early work. If I did, then I am honoured, for today Simon quite clearly is ranked with that relatively small number of top wildlife artists who are accepted as being internationally supreme in this highly specialised field – those artists who paint the environment and wildlife with not only complete competence, but tremendous knowledge and, perhaps most important of all, feeling and compassion for wildlife.

David Shepherd OBE
Surrey

AUTHOR'S ACKNOWLEDGEMENTS

I am indebted to Clive Holloway, firstly for conceiving the idea of this book, and secondly, through his persistence, interest and diplomatic bullying, for turning my initial scepticism into wholehearted enthusiasm.

Special thanks go to my wife, Susie, who with love and understanding coped calmly and patiently with the metamorphosis from easy-going, even-tempered painter to distant, monosyllabic, irritable writer.

I am grateful to Dave Usher and his Greenwich Workshop staff for invaluable support and advice, not only in the compilation of this book, but over the past ten years of our happy association.

In the early stages of my painting career, Game Conservation International were infinitely supportive and encouraging. To them, and Paula McGeehee particularly for her help with this book, I am deeply appreciative.

Many of my safaris and my field work would not have been possible without the help and companionship of my good friend Alan Binks, to whom I am sincerely grateful. Similarly, to Nigel Pavitt and Ian McKenzie-Vincent for their expert assistance.

Finally, to my many friends who own the paintings displayed in this book, I extend my thanks for permitting their reproduction.

LEOPARD DOZING IN SUNLIGHT

As far back as I can remember, animals and nature have been an obsession. The Dorset countryside where I was born was filled with birds, small animals and exciting creepy-crawlies, most of which I tried unsuccessfully to capture; the few that were unlucky were carried home triumphantly, there to be condemned to a jam jar or cardboard box until they either expired from excessive attention, or were secretly released by my mother when she felt my interest was flagging.

One of my earliest and most loved pets was a caterpillar. Shortly after its capture, I took it in a jam jar with a string handle to show our nearest neighbour, a farmer with the wonderful name of Puckett, but somehow the jar tipped over and the precious caterpillar escaped into Mr Puckett's muck heap. I recall running home with an empty jar bawling my head off. Apparently my anguish was so great that my mother, Mr Puckett and all his farm hands spent the rest of the morning unsuccessfully turning the muck heap upside-down. Eventually, Mr Puckett's son was ordered to find a replacement and in time a bigger and better caterpillar was installed safely in the jar. I have often thought that this silly story would be a limerick writer's dream, particularly using one or two words which must have been muttered that morning to rhyme with some of the principal characters in the drama.

Forty-two years after this incident, I was waiting in fear and trepidation for the opening of my first major one-man exhibition in the United States when a card arrived from my mother in Nairobi. It read: "When you were two you bashed a mass of dots onto a piece of paper with your pencil and proudly announced that they were ants. From that day I knew you would be an artist." What faith and imagination. She must have wondered in the interim years whether her vision would ever materialise.

My father returned from the war in 1945 to find, as the youngest son, an unpromising future on the family farm. Accordingly, he applied to join a government scheme to acquire land and settle in Kenya and, early the following year, set off to stake his claim and make ready a home for the rest of us. Some months later we sailed from Southampton on a troop ship, my three-year-old brother suffering from whooping cough, my heavily pregnant mother, my diminutive but formidable grandmother and me. It must have been hell for the adults but it was a wonderful adventure for a small boy.

We arrived in Mombasa and boarded a train for the two-day journey to Nakuru, a small town in the Great Rift Valley. After leaving the coastal strip, we travelled endless miles through the Taru desert, a flat expanse of "wait-a-bit" thorn teeming with wildlife, particularly elephants. Then on through what is now the Tsavo National Park, with herds of buffalo and antelope, wildebeest and giraffe; on again to the Athi plains, alive with Thompson's and Grant's gazelles. Many years passed before I took that train again, and by that time the journey had come to be customarily undertaken by night. This has been a perennial puzzle for my memory: how could I have seen all those animals if it was dark? I have been forced to assume that the train did run in daytime during that first African journey, for it certainly left an indelible picture in my mind.

Our first home comprised a group of mud and wattle rondavels with thatched roofs and dirt floors, linked together by sheltered walkways. There was no running water, no electricity and the food was cooked on an open fire in one of the huts. Within the first year my father had built a proper stone house with a good shingle roof and proper plumbing. It was a beautiful house built on high ground in the centre of the farm, surrounded by elegant flat-topped acacia trees and with wonderful views, looking to the north down the Solai valley, and to the east towards the towering escarpment of the Rift Valley wall.

The farm itself was not large by Kenya standards and the area had been settled for some years so there was some degree of development. Consequently, wildlife was comparatively scarce but still prolific by English standards. It was not long before I had explored the length and breadth of our eight hundred acres. Along the western boundary ran a stream in a deep, forested gorge and here I discovered monkeys, baboons, bushbuck, duiker, wild pig, porcupines, otters and many other small animals. Here too were less pleasant characters: African bees which taught me an early and painful lesson, huge pythons, cobras and puff adders, and several species of potent nettle.

The area was renowned for its snakes. I remember watching delightedly while my grandmother, who was a trained nurse, treated with Fitzimmons' Snakebite Outfit a labourer who had been bitten on the leg by a puff adder, a snake similar in shape, looks and reputation to a rattlesnake. The Africans held their own respectful beliefs about snakes and this poor man, grey and shaking with fear, was convinced he would die. However, he survived and Grandma's stock in trade soared.

Not too many miles away was the huge, extinct Menengai volcano and the surrounding countryside showed much evidence of the volcano's past life. The farm was riddled with huge holes, some of indeterminate depth, some as much as thirty yards in diameter, choked with a tangle of undergrowth and huge boulders. The Africans feared them saying that they were bottomless and that a person or animal falling in would never be seen again. To add spice to their story, they told me that huge snakes lived down in the depths. Despite these warnings I was drawn to the crater cracks, as they were called, and managed to climb down to quite a depth – though never out of sight of daylight – and never did I find the fabled snake. I treated them with greater respect after the big storm when inches of rain fell on the farm in just a few hours and a raging brown torrent of flood water roared along the valley below our house. I followed my father to see where it was going and watched in awe as thousands and thousands of gallons disappeared into a crater crack.

Wherever I went I was followed constantly at a discreet distance by a ragged band of semi-naked black *totos* (children), the sons of my father's labourers. It was not long before we established communication and became firm friends and allies. In a short time I could pronounce a few words in Swahili and in their own language, Kipsigis.

At first they must have wondered how a kid could be so stupid. I had no idea how to hunt or trap animals and birds or what to do with them if I succeeded, but I learned fast and could soon compete adequately. There was so much to learn: which wood made the best bow, which bush the best arrows, how to cut and fasten the flights, how to forge an arrowhead from a five-inch nail and then how to shoot. I learned to make and set a dozen different kinds of trap. We made catapults and spears and *rungus* (clubs); and then we practised and practised, devising games to test our accuracy.

THE NOMADS

This was the painting which I completed in my "bush studio" on the banks of the Mara River; the one which was smudged when a furious mother elephant chased a pride of lions through my camp.

I called it "The Nomads", for this is what they are; two young males, too old to remain in the pride where they would threaten the authority of the dominant male, and too young to challenge for a pride of their own. So they are forced to lead a nomadic existence wandering the fringes of established pride territories and learning survival the hard way. They are probably full brothers, inseparable now but quite likely to fight viciously at some future time when a lioness takes their fancy.

DIKDIK

The dainty dikdik is almost the smallest African antelope, being little larger than a domestic cat. They mate for life, each pair having a strict territory in which there are specific areas where they defecate.

Once upon a time the king, queen and baby dikdik were walking through the bush when junior, frolicking ahead, fell into a pile of elephant dung and suffocated. A royal decree was subsequently issued to the effect that from henceforth all dikdiks would dump their tiny pellets in one spot in the vengeful hope that one day a pile would grow big enough to get an elephant. That is why one always finds dikdiks doing it in the same spot. (Authentic African legend.)

Not content with our weapons, we also had the use of a strange assemblage of dogs: the *totos*' numerous half-starved pi-hounds cringed beside my family's disdainful great dane, our tough and ugly bull terrier-cross-bulldog bitch and our two excitable nearly-Sealyham terriers.

When the whole show got on the road, you might think it a miracle that anything survived. On the other hand, the amount of noise we made gave any potential prey fair warning of our approach, and our successes were limited; but we had fun.

I happily became a collector. My bedroom was cluttered with stones, feathers, skulls, snake skins, pressed flowers, knives, birds' eggs, pinned moths and butterflies. In addition to the inanimate collections were live treasures: insects, lizards, snakes, tortoises, mice and birds. Few of these lasted for long and the intensity of the tantrum following each escape or death was in direct proportion to the assumed rarity of the specimen.

One of my blackest fits of fury was caused by the escape of a tortoise. It was no ordinary tortoise. I had been riding my bicycle down a bush path some miles from home when I spotted him/her plodding along stolidly in the long grass. It was huge, at least 18 inches high; I had to take it home if it killed me. Close to the path was an eroded gully into which I wheeled the bike to a position were the seat was on the same level as the tortoise. Then, pushing and shoving, I manoeuvred the monster off the edge and neatly onto the cycle seat where it balanced delicately, legs waving frantically, hissing in fury and emitting unimaginably pungent streams of pee.

It took an age to wheel the bicycle out of the gully without upsetting its precious load and many hours to teeter home, but I made it and showed off my new find with triumph and pride. The giant was consigned to the existing tortoise run in the garden but, to be on the safe side, I drilled a hole near the edge of its shell and tied it to a stake on a long cord. A few hours later it was gone. Like a battle tank it had uprooted the stake and ploughed effortlessly out of the enclosure, never to be seen again.

One day a calf went missing. Initially it was assumed to have been stolen, but a few days later another went and the remains of its carcass were found high in the fork of a tree. Leopard! My father sought the advice of a neighbour experienced in these matters and, in due course, a small hut was built out of stout saplings, with one small, two-foot-high doorway. A sacrificial goat was tethered inside the hut and a high-powered rifle positioned, muzzle pointing downwards above the door. A trip wire ran from the trigger down the side of the door and across the gap some twelve inches from the ground.

I watched these preparations in fascination and felt great sadness for the goat as the trap was primed at dusk and we moved away, hearing its pathetic bleats fade into the distance.

At dawn the next day, trembling with excitement and apprehension, I drove with my father to the little hut, having been told by the men that a shot had been heard in the night. Dad stopped the car thirty yards away, loaded his shotgun with SSG and very gingerly approached the trap. No goat. No leopard. But there was some blood. Evidently the door had been just too big and the cat had been winged. It was a tense and nerve-racking morning for poor Dad as he cautiously searched the thick bush for hours. The blood trail petered out and neither leopard nor goat was ever found.

Unfortunately, my idyllic life on the farm was not continuous. Shortly after our arrival in Kenya I was sent away to boarding school and, from the moment I set foot in the place, hated and loathed it with a passion. There was a polyglot mixture of nationalities including Afrikaners, Italians and Greeks, some of whom spoke no English. The *lingua franca* was Swahili. Others had missed out on early schooling and were therefore several years older than their classmates. Bullying was rife. Discipline was severe, the smallest infringement resulting in a beating. I was small for my age, with a mop of angelic, curly hair, and spoke insufficient Swahili, so the first year was unmitigated hell.

By far the worst tribulation was the food, which was little better than pig swill, but every morsel had to be eaten, otherwise – the cane. Like my own son now, I was a fussy eater and swallowing some foods was a physical impossibility. The alternative to a daily beating was to fill my handkerchief surreptitiously with the inedible bits: lumpy porridge, semolina, tapioca and gristly meat. This soggy bundle was then stuffed in my pocket until we were allowed to leave the dining-hall. Then it would be fed to one of the many semi-wild cats which prowled outside.

Above all, the school taught me survival. I could not possibly defend myself physically, so it was imperative to join one of the many "gangs" where a united force would deter would-be bullies. This could only be achieved by mute invitation after the members had been duly impressed by some act of strength or daring. Then it might be permitted for me to follow meekly in their protective wake.

I set my sights on a group whose core comprised four uncompromising, tough brothers. Their father was a game-trapper, catching animals for zoos all over the world, and stories of their holiday exploits left me goggle-eyed with envy and admiration. They kept (illicitly) a number of exotic pets and, like me, were enthusiastic collectors of birds' eggs.

My chance came one day when a crows' nest was discovered at the top of a mighty eucalyptus tree. Nobody had a prized crow's egg in their collection and no-one, it seemed, could scale that massive trunk. If I could do nothing else, I could climb trees and so duly I staked my membership on this seemingly impossible feat. I don't know how I did it. I can still remember vividly the agony and terror of that climb, the incredible sense of triumph and achievement at reaching the nest with its stench of carrion and droppings, stuffing two large blue-green eggs into my mouth, looking down and seeing a great crowd of silent boys watching, and realising that the most difficult part was still to come – getting down. I made it, shaking, scratched and bleeding but bursting with pride as I disgorged the still-intact eggs from my mouth. Congratulations rang like music in my ears and I was accepted.

After that, life became much easier and I revelled in my new friendships. On the other hand, I now had a reputation to live up to – if it's crazy enough, Combes will do it – but nothing ever again taxed me as much as the crows' nest incident. It was certainly a turning point, giving me great confidence and a feeling of belonging.

The brothers became very close friends and still are to this day. Through them my interest in wildlife blossomed and made me realize that what we had on the farm was very small game compared to the environment in which they lived. I listened keenly to their stories of elephants and lions, giraffes and buffalo, and longed to share such exciting experiences.

In the early fifties that wish, to some extent, came true, though partly through misfortune. It was a sad and turbulent time. First there was the shock of my father contracting polio, which left him with a shrivelled game leg. Through sheer determination he learned to walk again, but the gremlins were active, and a series of very unfortunate events forced him to sell our beloved farm: foot and mouth disease cut down the cattle; the crops failed; a large concrete tank, built at great expense to revolutionise the farm's water supply, was split in half one night by an earth tremor. To add to the general anxiety, this was a time of great political uncertainty as the Mau Mau rebellion developed. The British Army arrived in force and both my parents were obliged to carry weapons.

The farm had to be auctioned off. I thought the end of the world had come:

BEWARE THE INTRUDER

We almost missed him. Driving slowly past an isolated acacia tree near Seronera (Tanzania), the leopard's tail, dangling down from a dense mass of branches and foliage like a bell rope, just caught my eye – a subtle break in the natural pattern of the tree. Slowly, I eased the vehicle closer and for a long time sat watching just the tail and a few small patches of his golden coat. I sensed a restlessness amongst my fellow watchers, impatient for the sleepy cat to show himself so, drawing a deep breath, I let out a marginally passable imitation of a leopard's roar. This is not really a roar – it sounds more like someone sawing wood. The result was gratifyingly spectacular. The leopard bounded across the tree from his hiding place until he was almost above the car and stared threateningly over our heads into the distance.

BUFFALO HERD

I remember seeing a painting, possibly by Künhert, depicting a herd of black cape buffalo standing in bleached yellow grass. I was enthralled by the dramatic contrast in colours and embarked on this piece with the recollection strongly in my mind. To accentuate the contrast even further, I silhouetted the milling herd against a background of swirling, sunlit dust; but something more was needed so I created the giant tree rising almost too symmetrically out of the dust like a huge peacock tail. On reflection, I wished I had used a larger canvas because the outcome lost some of its effect in a smaller format.

When I was a boy, a buffalo sighting was rare. I believe it was the devastating effects of rinderpest which had decimated the herds. Twenty-five years later, when this painting was on the easel, it was possible to see herds of a thousand animals – an example of the remarkable population fluctuations and regenerative powers of the animals of Africa.

no more hunting, no more adventures. But then one day we were loaded into our ancient box-body Chev and told we were going to see the place where Dad had been offered a job. An hour's drive, and we arrived at the entrance to Soysambu, a 50,000-acre ranch owned by Lord Delamere, who had asked Father to take over as dairy cattle manager.

As we drove through the ranch, my mood changed rapidly from dismal resignation to supercharged excitement. It was big, it was wild and everywhere I looked, there were animals. There were rivers and cliffs, plains and mountains, and a ten-mile-long lake fringed with pink flamingoes. I prayed he would take it, and he did. A week later all our belongings, including cats and dogs, were piled into a truck and transported to our new home situated on a bluff overlooking the lake. I was back in heaven.

I was twelve years old at the time of this move and ready to progress to a secondary boarding school, the Duke of York School in Nairobi. I had shown little interest in sport and academically I was merely average, but I was good at art and spent many hours during the holidays carving, modelling, drawing and painting.

The next five years were the best that any teenage boy could have wished for. This was not on account of the new school, for although it was a vast improvement on the old one my hatred of educational authority had become ingrained. However, this inconvenience was more than made up for by the holidays at Soysambu. Shortly after our arrival there, I was taken to a Kenya-style children's party. Not for them Blind-Man's-Buff or Grandmother's Footsteps – we had a shooting competition. Bottles were lined up on a gate and each boy invited to knock them down. I scored most and, to my complete delight and amazement, was given the rifle as a prize. It was a ten-shot, pump-action .22 and would be my constant companion for many years to come.

Looking back now, I must have been a worry to my parents. With the Mau Mau becoming ever more violent, I would disappear with my rifle and a couple of dogs, only reappearing occasionally to eat or sleep. Much of the time I had a minder, Arap Soi, a lean Kipsigis tribesman who could run and run and run; he was a natural athlete, who was seldom without a wicked grin on his face.

Under Soi's tutelage it soon became apparent that the skills I had picked up from the *totos* at Solai were really very amateurish and inadequate. Soysambu was no place for kids' games. It covered a vast area ranging in altitude from 5,000 to 9,000 feet and was home to some large and potentially dangerous wild animals. No longer was I a small boy hurling rocks at hares and shooting birds with a toy bow and arrow; now I had a rifle and the chance to go for much bigger game.

In retrospect, I have often tried to analyse my passion for hunting during those teenage years. Why did I get such a kick out of killing animals? I do remember frequently feeling a fleeting sense of remorse but never enough to stop me doing the same thing the next day.

Firstly, I think it was the excitement and challenge of the chase. I prided myself on being able, in most instances, to drop my quarry with a single shot; with a small calibre rifle this often necessitated a long and patient stalk to within very close range. I believe that most young men perhaps have a latent instinct to hunt and dominate the environment in which they live. In my case, all the ingredients were there for me to indulge those instincts.

Secondly, I cannot remember any moral restrictions. I was not conscious of any fervent desire to conserve, wild animals were plentiful, there was no television to bring us the wonderful wildlife documentaries that we see today and the talk amongst my peers on the ranch and at school was all of hunting. I hero-worshipped the legendary hunters of earlier times and avidly read every book about them that I could find.

One of these legendary figures, by then an old man, lived close by. F.H. Clarke had been a famous elephant hunter until, reputedly, he lost his nerve and retired to an ugly little house built to his own peculiar tastes. All the window panes were painted over so that he lived in an atmosphere of almost total seclusion and eccentricity. Disdainful of the modern china toilet with its fancy wooden seat, he built a simple, severe concrete bowl onto which he lowered his considerable, naked bulk whilst the cement was still wet to ensure that the shape moulded exactly to his specifications. The walls of the house were adorned with hundreds of old photographs of his hunting exploits and heads of his trophies, and every piece of furniture was covered with priceless skins. If I were to see such a place now I would think it grotesque, but at that age it was a treasure house. His pride and joy was a full-sized snooker table which was the only reason we children were permitted into his holy of holies – my father was his favourite snooker partner.

The urge to hunt stayed with me until my mid-twenties when suddenly I lost all interest. At about the same time I started drawing and painting; could this have been a substitute? Certainly it was not a deliberate transition – it just happened.

Whatever the moral judgement on my hunting activities, there is no question that I could never have achieved a finer grounding for a career as a wildlife painter. To hunt successfully it is necessary to have an intimate knowledge of the quarry. I could spend a whole hour stalking a herd of impala, watching intently their every move, their mood, their attitude, their social interaction. After the kill, I had to skin and butcher the animals so here were valuable lessons in anatomy although, at the time, I had no idea that one day this knowledge would be of use.

Lake Elmenteita lay at the lowest point of the ranch on its north-eastern boundary. The land rose to the south of the lake in a series of plateaux like huge steps, each plateau ending in a steep cliff. Beyond the highest point the ground sloped away gradually across a great, open, treeless plain where many herds of Grant's and Thompson's gazelles, impalas and zebras could be found. The wooded valleys of the two streams that fed the lake contained bushbuck, monkeys, baboons, bush pig and leopard. East of the lake was an ancient caldera surrounded by a nightmarish, twisted tangle of old lava choked with impenetrable undergrowth. This was the wild end of the ranch, where buffalo, eland, lion and even rhino were sometimes seen.

Our house was situated about a mile south of the lake adjacent to one of the cliffs which started as a jumble of huge boulders just a few minutes' walk from our back door. After a twenty-minute walk along the cliff one reached its highest point – some six hundred feet from the plateau below – and here was my eyrie. A deep crack about a yard wide split the cliff from top to bottom. The upper end of this fissure was blocked by the tangled roots of a huge wild fig tree which clung to the rock like a giant octopus. Some three yards below the tree was a large ledge, accessible only by wriggling into the crack and clinging to the tree roots.

FLAMINGO STUDY

It was a wonderful hideaway, invisible to anyone above or below, yet offering the most spectacular views across the valley, where the two streams meandered into the lake, and beyond that to the distant range of hills where tiny vehicles travelled the main Nairobi to Nakuru road. To the right was the lake itself, with its fringe of pink flamingoes and, thirty miles away in the distance, the peak of Mount Longonot.

The cliff was home to families of rock hyrax, baboons, monkeys, multi-coloured lizards, swallows, swifts, augur buzzards and eagles. Amongst the scattered boulders and scrub below were dikdik, duiker, mountain reedbuck, mongooses, several species of small cat and a multitude of different birds.

HEADING FOR WATER

A line of elephants moving to water in the height of the dry season makes me want to reach for the nearest cold Tusker beer. Every step they take appears to require great effort and heads, trunks, ears and tails seem to droop with exhaustion as each plate-sized foot flops to the ground raising its own dust cloud. The pace increases the closer they get to the water and the last few yards may be taken at a run. Now, visibly, they come to life as gallons of life-giving liquid are sucked up trunks and squirted into mouths. Having slaked their thirst, they will spray their overheated skins first with water and then with dust. Years of this daily treatment will impregnate their hides with the local soil colour. These elephants have the characteristic light grey colouring of Amboseli where the soil is, in parts, almost white.

CHEETAH PAIR

These two male cheetahs were in their absolute prime and probably full brothers. They will hunt together and amicably share a kill unlike their ill-mannered cousins, the lions. Nothing is more exciting to watch than a cheetah hunting. Within a few paces it will reach a speed of 40 mph and can cover a hundred yards in three seconds. The powerful hindlegs reach far forward crossing beyond the forelegs as the animal's back hunches; then a mighty thrust, the forelegs reaching far forward, the body elongates and changes from convex to concave thanks to specially adapted "hinges" in the vertebral column which allow maximum reach. As the cheetah closes, its prey zigzags frantically in its desperation to escape. The cat follows, using its tail for a counterbalance as it negotiates each change of direction. Finally, the cheetah's front paw shoots forward in a skilful feat of balance, tripping its prey; a tangle of legs and bodies, a cloud of dust and the gazelle is gripped by the throat. All over in seconds.

This was my den, my home, my battle headquarters, my retreat, my island. Here I dreamed, planned, fantasised, observed, studied, absorbed and ruled my kingdom. In this holy of holies I would not shoot anything and, in time, as the inhabitants became accustomed to my presence, I revelled in their proximity and trust.

It was here, at the age of fourteen, that I hatched my master plan, deciding that school and civilisation as such were a dead loss, that I would run away and live in the bush forever. Most boys of this age would be saving their money for a bicycle or radio. Not me. During the following year, I spent every penny I could get on ammunition, maps, fishing tackle, knives, string, salt, sugar and general survival equipment. I spent hours drawing plans of the house I would build in the forest and of the water supply system I would install, and designing the traps I would need and the clothes I would make from skins.

Towards the end of that year, after careful vetting, I confided my plan in my closest school friend, who decided to join me in my escape. We pooled our resources and I felt a bit better that now I would have company and support. We fixed a date for our departure during the school holidays, when he would come to stay at the ranch, we would assemble our store of supplies and then we would quietly disappear. Everything went according to plan until, shortly before D-day, I began to realise how terribly I would miss my dogs, home, parents, brother and sister – not necessarily in that order. After great heart-searchings, guilt, self-recrimination and shame at being so weak, I told my friend I could not go through with it. I'm sure he never forgave me.

At Soysambu our house became a zoo. Hyrax (rock rabbits) were my favourite pets – small, soft animals, easily house-trained, affectionate and intelligent. They slept in my bed cuddling up to me for warmth, uttering little grunts and squeaks to communicate their happiness and contentment. Unfortunately, they had a passion for rose leaves, so Mother's carefully nurtured roses were constantly defoliated.

Our flock of Muscovy ducks were host to a succession of beautiful Egyptian geese which were caught, before they could fly, in the lucerne fields by the lake. As soon as they matured they flew back to the lake, undoubtedly to breed more goslings to keep our Muscovies company.

Out in the chicken house, carefully separated from the ever panic-stricken hens by a wire netting partition, lived three young augur buzzards which had been brought in as hungry but fiercely defiant balls of fluff. Thanks to an army of *totos* who produced daily rations of field rats at ten cents a tail, the young buzzards thrived and grew eventually to maturity when, reluctantly, I released them. At one stage I had aspirations to train them to hunt, but nothing would persuade them against the easy option of the ever-present rat supply.

YOUNG HYRAX

Reluctantly, with much physical persuasion and verbal abuse, they would fly a short distance, only to return, if I was lucky, to my gauntlet-protected arm, but more often to my unprotected shoulder or head. In time they were urged to go free but spent several weeks roosting on the roof of our house, terrorising our flock of domestic pigeons, not to mention all the other birds in the neighbourhood.

A succession of duikers, dikdiks and Thompson's gazelles lived in my bedroom. Most of these animals were brought to me by the Africans, often very young, half starved, with their legs tied to prevent escape and always terrified. The mortality rate was high but occasionally one would survive and thrive; then it was fascinating to watch their behaviour and that of our large dogs which, outside the boundaries of the garden, would chase anything that moved, but inside knew that everyone had to coexist. The little antelopes seemed to sense our protection and know that dire consequences would result for any dog which so much as uttered a growl at them. Walking as if on tiptoe on their tiny hooves, struggling for traction on the shiny floors, they would put their heads down and mock charge the nearest dog which, in turn, would writhe with embarrassment and skulk off, head and tail down, to a more secluded spot where the maintenance of self-control was not so essential.

Once I had a vervet monkey. Joey was a tyrant and, to me, a real challenge. I always prided myself on being able to tame any animal by winning its trust and confidence, but Joey was a biter and sly one at that. When, at last, I thought I could handle him with relative safety, he would lull me into a sense of false security and then, quite unexpectedly, sink his teeth into my hand. One day when he was doing just that and concentrating hard on the job, I sank my own teeth into his tail. The effect was remarkable. He leapt round and faced me; eyes wide and aggressive but with his little mouth open in seeming astonishment; then he settled submissively onto my arm and started grooming me. Never again did he bite me. Although he would lunge open-mouthed and grab my finger in his teeth he would never actually clamp his jaws shut. However, woe betide anyone else who tried to handle him.

For a brief but embarrassing period, Joey became a star. A small film unit moved into our house to use the ranch as a location for the making of a children's wildlife movie. I was co-opted to provide various small animals including a monkey, and on the appointed day we took him to the acacia forest near the lake where he was to perform his short, simple part. Unfortunately, he escaped and spent the entire day a hundred feet up a huge yellow acacia tree, being roundly and comprehensively abused by the entire film crew. I added more than a few unmentionable words to my forbidden vocabulary.

One breathtaking addition to my menagerie was a pair of crowned cranes which arrived as gangly, grey, fluffy fledglings, wearing a ridiculous tuft on top of their heads and an expression of constant astonishment. Like a pair of tropical ugly ducklings

VERVET MONKEY

MARTIAL EAGLE

Whoever named the martial eagle was right on target. Everything from its fierce yellow eyes to its supreme efficiency as a hunter are aptly applied to the word martial, with its connotations of conflict and attrition. I have watched these fearsome raptors kill mongooses, monkeys, gazelles and snakes, carrying their quarry into nearby trees but, more often than not, being unable to fly with the weight of it. In that event, they spread their wings over the prey (mantling), shielding it from the prying eyes of airborne scavengers before dragging it under cover of the nearest bush. In this instance the prey is a puff adder probably weighing about eight pounds.

ZEBRAS AT THE WATER HOLE

From a painting point of view, I have an obsession with zebras and water and will spend many hours watching, sketching and photographing this daily event when the herds come to drink. The bold markings appear in such contrast to the greens and browns along the water's edge but the most exciting and satisfying task is painting the water itself. Any water is a challenge – minute and subtle highlights can suddenly produce such liquidity, sparkle and depth but the addition of a zebra's reflection seems to bring even more vibrance to the subject especially if, as is normally the case, the water is disturbed.

they grew into the most beautiful birds and attached themselves to my grandmother, with whom a mutual love/hate relationship was established. When she emerged from her room to feed the cranes they would bounce enthusiastically towards her, huge wings outspread, clamouring for her hand-out and deftly dodging her furiously brandished walking stick.

Most of our collection of dogs joined us from the ranks of local waifs and strays, or those that were simply looking for a new home. An exception was a brindled boxer pup which I believe was actually bought for money. She was a puppy of boundless energy but limited intelligence, both characteristics coming to the fore when she decided that a seven-foot spitting cobra was worth a game. We were on a track a mile or so from home when she found the snake, which soon reared up with hood spread as the idiot puppy ran around it in circles, barking and lunging. In desperation I crouched and reached forward, grabbing a back leg to wrench her out of harm's way but, in doing so, glanced up in time to see an evil mouth spring open and a spray of venom hit my face. I threw myself backwards, still clutching the dog, unable to see a thing as the poison burned my eyes, wondering frantically where the snake was. When I reckoned I had backed off a safe distance I tried to control my rising panic; how long did I have before the poison destroyed my sight and which way was home? I was still on the track and, as it was quite early in the morning, I could feel the direction of the sun. Hoping that the cobra had disappeared, I set off, holding the dog in my arms for the first few hundred yards to stop her running back to the snake. I managed to feel my way along the track, knowing I was off course when I touched long grass or the ditch.

I have no idea how long I walked before some Africans found me and rushed me home. I was laid on my back in the bath and milk was poured into my eyes until at last the pain began to subside. For the next two weeks I stayed in a darkened room until I could stand the light, and for a long time afterwards any strong light would leave my eyes sore and watering. From that time I developed a mild snake phobia.

Zebras were considered a pest at the far end of the ranch, not only because they were suspected of carrying disease, but because a large herd would demolish a five-strand, high-tension fence. I discovered that it was possible to borrow a .303 rifle from the Elmenteita police station to shoot zebra. However, I had no intention of doing that; instead, I wanted to shoot a buffalo. The rifle I borrowed was first war vintage and had a simple leaf-aperture rear sight with the apertures corresponding to two ranges – 200 or 500 yards. Looking through either aperture it was possible to see not only the foresight but a great deal of Africa too, so I stuck a piece of black paper over the hole and pierced it with a safety pin before zeroing the rifle with two out of the handful of precious rounds with which I had been issued.

I knew it was highly risky to attempt to shoot a buffalo with such an old, low-calibre rifle, but I was banking on being able to creep up very close. The buffalo lived near the lake shore in a wicked piece of country basically consisting of an ancient lava flow. Between the ridges of crumbling, black, jagged rocks were small hollows in which grew tightly-packed, tangled thickets of thorn and ten-foot tall bamboo grass. I had hoped to follow the ridge tops and look down on my quarry, but it was impossible to walk quietly on the loose rock, and the undergrowth in the hollows was too thick to allow a view of any animals. After several attempts which resulted only in crashing, unseen buffalo stampedes somewhere in the thicket, Soi and I decided we would have to get right down to their level to achieve any real success.

THREE GENERATIONS

Buffalo have the reputation for being the meanest of animals. As far as hunters are concerned, this is justified since more have been killed by them than by any other animal species. I have hunted buffalo with friends on private land where, in the past, they were unwelcome as carriers of cattle disease. I was never successful but

can vividly recall the heart-thumping tension as we crawled through dense bush with stories of the buffalo's tenacity, intelligence, ferocity and cunning foremost in my mind; how they will double back on their tracks to wait in ambush, then charge the unsuspecting pursuer from the rear; how, even when mortally wounded, their massive reserves of adrenalin will sustain their momentum for an improbably long time.

Even now, in the parks and reserves where most species have become inured to tourist traffic, the buffalo seems to retain its uncompromising attitude to all and sundry.

LEOPARD ROCK

How many millions of years did it take for the leopard to evolve into the beautifully marked super-cat that we see, albeit fleetingly, today? Perhaps a mere flicker in time compared to the age of these venerable granite boulders from the kopjes of Serengeti. Scientists speculate that these are some of the world's oldest rocks, dating back two to three billion years in time. These kind of statistics are almost too much for me to comprehend. What changes have they witnessed over all those aeons? Probably, they will still be there when man and all his mad machinations have become a mere puff of dust in the passage of time.

Buffalo communications through the bamboo grass were by way of tunnels along which it was necessary either to stoop or crawl. Visibility was limited to a few yards and the strong, bovine stink of the animals added to our nervousness and tension as we crept forward. Suddenly, there was a loud snort and the crash of undergrowth at frighteningly close range. In an instant I realised that the herd was coming towards us, so I forced my way frantically into the side of the tunnel just as the first huge, black body came hurtling past. All thoughts of shooting disappeared as self-preservation became paramount and I burrowed deeper into my hideaway. At last they were all past and, as the thunder of hooves and snapping of branches faded, Soi and I scrambled out into the open, shaking with relief and vowing to give up buffalo hunting.

We owned an old black labrador perversely named Swan. One evening he failed to turn up at feeding time which was most unusual for, even if he was courting, Swan never forgot his stomach. Days went by with still no sign of the old dog and we feared the worst. Dogs are a delicacy for leopards and several had disappeared in the area in recent months.

Some weeks later I was moving silently through the thick bush at the base of a cliff looking for wild bee hives when I glanced up to see a large leopard crouched flat on top of a huge boulder watching me intently. As soon as he realised he had been spotted, the big cat melted away leaving me futilely clutching my little .22 with heart thumping.

At that time my shelf was stocked with books by the legendary big game hunters and I was an avid reader of Rider Haggard, and of Jim Corbett's tales of India (including the one about the man-eating leopard of Rudraprayag). The hairs on the back of my neck began to prickle as I recalled stories of the leopard's cunning and stealth, its speed and ferocity if cornered or in defence of its young; maybe there were cubs hidden close by. Was it not best to lie flat on the ground if a leopard charged? Never look it in the eye. The .22 was useless; could I use my hunting knife if it actually charged? What about the theory that if you held on to its tongue it couldn't bite? Never show fear … maybe I should whistle or sing …

Nervously, I looked at the thick bush surrounding me on three sides and then at the broken cliff face on the fourth – that was the way out. As I crept closer to the rocks, convinced that a pair of cold yellow eyes was tracking my every move, I became aware of an overhang which formed a small, shallow cave at the base of the cliff. The dry, dusty floor was littered with bones and unidentified droppings and the air reeked of bats and musty decay. Expecting any minute to hear a growl of fury, I eased cautiously away and started climbing, relief flooding over me as I moved higher and further from the sinister menace below.

Reaching the top, I sat down feeling rather foolish for being such a drip. I scanned the thick bush below hoping to catch a glimpse of the leopard and then, some distance away in open ground, I noticed something dark hanging from the branches of a tree. It had to be a leopard's kill, possibly a goat or a calf, but I convinced myself that it was Swan.

Revenge and retribution. I raced home and immediately poured out the story of this discovery to Soi whose eyes lit up with excitement. He told me how we would hunt it the next day.

In the morning, when Father had left the house, I took his 12-bore shotgun from the cupboard and a handful of LG and SSG cartridges from the drawer before joining Soi, a gang of his cronies all armed to the teeth with spears, bows and arrows and *simis* (short double-bladed swords) and a yapping, excited pack of pi-dogs. I was given an old blanket and instructed to wrap it round my left arm when we reached leopard country. If it charged I was to thrust my blanket covered arm at its mouth.

For some time we moved noisily along the base of the cliff encouraging the dogs. The kill in the tree was indeed the dried-out remains of Swan so that mystery, at least, had been solved. Soon the tenor of barking changed perceptibly and I was sure I heard the deep, guttural growl of the leopard. We rushed forward, silent now, adrenalin pumping, each one wondering what the next few minutes would bring. Evidently, from the rising crescendo of barking, the dogs had bayed something up. It was in a dense thicket close to the cliff face surrounded by huge boulders that had fallen from the cliff centuries before. On hands and knees we crawled through the undergrowth until we could see the excited pack jumping and snarling at the base of a wild fig tree from whose lower branches came a long, deep, spine-chilling growl. I inched closer and caught a glimpse of wide, angry yellow eyes, ears laid flat and a face contorted with fury. It was magnificent. I struggled to disentangle myself from the undergrowth and aim the shotgun but as soon as the leopard saw us it sprang higher up the tree to the accompaniment of renewed, frenzied barking from below. Seeing it flee gave me fresh courage and I struggled closer to try and get a shot. High in the fig tree the leopard paused and seemed to look down disdainfully on the noisy rabble below. At the same time as I raised the gun I marvelled at its beauty and strength and glorious arrogance. I fired both barrels in quick succession, missed the target completely and, I think, deliberately, and watched in secret admiration as the cat sprang from a high branch across to a jutting rock on the cliff, on up and out of sight.

The experiences of that day confirmed me irrevocably as a "cat man". I had always loved and admired cats for their independence, stealth, beauty and hunting prowess and also envied them their ability to seem so comfortable and relaxed. However, having stared into those furious eyes and witnessed the lithe and graceful ease with which it had eluded its noisy, ham-fisted pursuers, I knew I had seen the ultimate cat. When I started painting animals, I concentrated through preference on the big cats and top of my list, perversely, was always the leopard. I say perversely because not only is it the most elusive to find but painting it is extremely time-consuming work, for putting in all those beautiful spots and rosettes is truly a labour of love.

Not all my time was spent hunting and roaming the plains. Lake Elmenteita lay at our doorstep demanding to be explored. Most of the shore was a wide, flat expanse of hard-packed, white encrusted soda. Fiercely hot and inhospitable, it was a different world from the one we lived in, just a few hundred feet higher in altitude. On the shore of the lake I found the bleached and battered remains of a boathouse positioned some distance from the water. Further enquiries revealed that the boat itself, a 12-foot aluminium dinghy, was hidden in reeds some distance away and the mast, sail, oars, rudder and centreboard were available at the general manager's house. In due course my brother Rob and I assembled all the components and set about teaching ourselves to sail.

It was a frustrating exercise. The water was very shallow, so that it was necessary to push or row several hundred yards out to find sufficient depth for the centreboard not to touch the bottom. Generally, the wind howled across the lake at fifteen to twenty knots with frequent sudden violent gusts, and always towards the shore where our moorings were. This meant that we had to tack to get away into deeper water and by the time we had the sail up and everything rigged, the wind had blown us back to a point where the centreboard dug into the mud. Even on the rare occasions that we actually

BUSHWHACKER

The romantic conception of a hunting leopard is a stealthy, ruthless, feline killer poised and hidden in the branches of a tree from where it springs silently onto the back of the hapless victim walking along the trail below. From the books I read as a boy, I entertained such notions with certain self-imposed standard operating procedures such as: if you see one in a tree, pretend you haven't and never look it in the eye. Boy's own stuff.

In reality, of course, the leopard seldom, if ever, hunts this way although stealth and cunning are foremost in its repertoire. He relies heavily on camouflage, ambush and infinite patience.

MIDDAY SIESTA

Lions are not preyed upon by any other animal, which probably explains their arrogance and lazy disregard for other species. Apparently, this also explains why they have no stripes or spots – no need for camouflage – although they do have spots when they are young. Resting during the day, they display strong family ties with much mutual rubbing, licking and body contact. Their uninterrupted life of sleeping, eating and breeding would suggest a population explosion but the illusion of peaceful cooperation disappears as soon as food is available. Then, survival of the fittest is the maxim. Recent apparent soul-mates spit and snarl and swipe at each other, and any lion not in top condition will go hungry without pricking the conscience of its fellows.

started moving under sail, our erratic zigzagging always seemed to push us backwards to where we started.

The lake water was alkaline so, after wading even for a short time, any part of the anatomy which chafed would be burnt raw. Pushing the boat was therefore an extremely uncomfortable undertaking. In the end we resigned ourselves to the fact that we could only sail competently with the wind directly behind us. Accordingly, we would wake before dawn, lug all the tackle down to the lake and start rowing before the sun was too hot and the wind too strong. By mid-morning we had reached the far end of the lake, after three or four hours' heaving at the oars. We took a rest, explored the surroundings, then climbed back on board, hoisted the sail and almost flew back to the other end. The exhilaration of that headlong run back was well worth the rowing effort.

We were both collectors of birds' eggs and it was whilst searching for these at the far end of the lake, close to a nesting colony of greater flamingoes, that we discovered a large, elaborate raft made from 44-gallon oil drums with a little house built on top. It was high and dry on the shore and apparently had not been used for some time. Finders keepers! We heaved it into the water and tied it behind our boat before heading for home, our usual lightning progress somewhat impeded this time by the weight of the raft.

The lake abounded with birds. Greater and lesser flamingoes flocked there in tens of thousands, not to mention a host of other indigenous and migrant waterfowl. Now that we had the raft we discovered that it was possible to approach very close, especially to flamingoes which were given to mass panic every time we used to approach on foot. We would sit and watch them for hours, rolling about helpless with laughter at their peculiar and clumsy social interaction and eccentric mannerisms. They were ludicrous to watch as they shuffled backwards to stir up the algae on which they fed, and then sieved it through their upside-down beaks. The most amusing antic, however, was when a seemingly sleeping flamingo, with head tucked under wing and one leg pulled up and concealed, would suddenly produce the hitherto unseen leg and frantically try to scratch its head which, in turn, remained cosily tucked away out of sight. The searching leg would wave around in the air desperately looking for a head to scratch until, invariably, the bird would fall over. Then, probably to divert attention from its loss of dignity, it would launch an attack on its nearest neighbour.

About a year later we heard that "our" raft was, in fact, a proper hide and belonged to the then Governor of the colony, who spent many weekends at Soysambu as a guest of Lord and Lady Delamere, indulging in his favourite pastime – birdwatching.

The Duke of York School in Nairobi proved a welcome improvement on my previous school (though I still counted the days until end of term). The change of schools, and perhaps the coincidental change of homes, seemed to bring about a considerable metamorphosis in me. From a small, weedy boy who really hated sport, suddenly I grew in all directions and developed a passion for athletics, rugby, hockey and shooting. Undoubtedly, my constant running and hunting during the school holidays contributed to my eventual winning of the open mile and the school shooting.

This athleticism seemed to bring a new group of friends, most of whom were hell-bent on breaking every rule in the school's book. The school was situated about ten miles from Nairobi, bounded on one side by forest reserve and on the other by the Kikuyu reservation, home of the tribe from which the Mau Mau originated. More than half of the school's extensive grounds comprised indigenous forest inhabited by many small animals and birds, not to mention

SERENGETI KOPJE

About a hundred years ago, a bird which had been feeding on the fruit of a wild fig tree flew across the Serengeti Plains and alighted on this kopje to rest or drink from one of its rain-filled, rocky depressions. A seed from the bird's droppings found the right conditions to germinate, possibly in the crook of an existing tree. Over the years the seedling grew, sending its aerial roots down and around its host until the original tree was strangled and died. Seeking more moisture the pale, tentacle-like roots grew further downwards, enveloping a huge boulder like a multi-fingered hand holding a ball. Overhead, the tree's large leaves spread a canopy of cool shade for heat-weary lions, cheetahs or leopards. Fruit bats by night and a multitude of birds by day feed from its fig-laden branches, and hyrax, lizards and wild bees occupy the many nooks and crannies created by the tree's tangled root system. For those with the patience to sit and watch, a fig tree is a wildlife treasure-house.

the occasional Mau Mau freedom fighter. Consequently, these areas were strictly out of bounds, but somehow we managed to sneak in there without getting caught.

The Mau Mau brought welcome relief to us boys from the routine of school life. We spent much of our time building sandbag and barbed wire fortifications round our dormitory blocks and every week or so the sirens would scream in the middle of the night; we always hoped it would be a real raid but, more often than not, it was just a practice as we leapt from our beds, hauled the mattress off and under the bed and then crawled under that clutching a formidable, stone-age type club with a six-inch nail protruding from the head. This was the authorised weapon for schoolboys. At this stage the Mau Mau were confined to the forests by the security forces and the few incidents at the school were simply attempts to acquire food and blankets.

Although it must have been of great concern to the school authorities and, of course, our parents, the consequences (for the school) of the Mau Mau rebellion, so important in Kenya's history, never really bothered us. There was much derogatory speculation as to where our teachers acquired their motley collection of weapons and whether some of the more nervous academics would know which end to point if the need should arise. Certainly, in my mother's case, the enemy would perhaps have died of laughter rather than any other cause. She kept a .32 Beretta in her handbag and if asked to produce it, would fumble lengthily through a tangled mass of personal effects muttering darkly that she had seen it there the other day. Finally, she would produce the weapon from the depths, triumphantly holding it by the trigger as a mixture of safety pins, hair grips and Eno's Fruit Salts trickled from the barrel. She and other local ladies would sometimes attend target practice firing at life sized cut-outs of a man and the instructor was both mystified and impressed when the majority of shots fell in an area some nine inches below the navel.

By the mid-fifties the security situation had eased, teachers no longer carried guns and we were allowed back into the forest. My interest in birds increased and I learned how to skin, cure and mount them to museum standards. The urge to catch animals and keep them as pets also continued, and my school acquisitions comprised mostly tree hyrax and bushbabies. However, my finest catch was a giant forest rat which measured over a yard from nose to tail. It was an extremely intelligent animal and became quite tame in just a few days, eating almost anything but smelling abominably. The only home I could find that was big enough to house this monster was my school trunk. At the end of term, with great reluctance, I set my giant rat free and filled my trunk with clothes before going home. My mother was perfectly horrified by the smell when she opened it.

One day we found a hive of wild bees in a hollow tree so, with polo-necked sweaters pulled up over our faces and held there by a tightly jammed on hat, socks over our hands and long trousers tucked into the socks on our feet, we hacked out the combs with a *panga* (*machete*), keeping the bees at bay with smoking grass. We gorged ourselves on honey and sold what we could not consume for a tidy profit.

At this time we were straying unlawfully beyond the school boundary into the forest reserve where many local Africans hung their traditional, hollow-log beehives in the trees. I discovered that, if the hive was dislodged, it would often split open when hitting the ground and most of the bees would then fly up to where it had hung. It was then a simple task to gather the combs and head back to school. It never crossed our foolish minds that we were stealing, but we were soon found out. In most African tribal law, a man's wife, cattle, sheep or crops are fair game but to take honey from his beehives is absolutely taboo. So it was that a delegation of local elders arrived at the school and

RHINO CHARGE

One part of a rhino's limited vocabulary sounds like a cross between a cat's mew and the bleat of a baby goat. It is not a difficult sound to produce and today's sadly depleted rhinos pay scant attention to the many two-legged vehicle-borne rhino bleaters who try to attract their attention. However, in the not too distant past, when these tetchy relics of a bygone age were in greater abundance, it was possible to encourage quite remarkable reactions with a few plaintive bleats.

This painting was a consequence of one such pseudo-conversation. The rhino raised his head and swung it from side to side seeking the scent of the invader of his territory. Then he wheeled and trotted towards me with his tail up, puffing and snorting. Now comes the crucial moment. Either you shut up and sit tight, in which case he may cautiously come close, realise you are not another rhino, and run away; or you issue the challenge. This comprises a series of loud, staccato snorts and raspberries which should be interpreted by the rhino as the ultimate insult and provoke a full-blooded charge. I leave you to guess which alternative I took here.

subsequently identified us as the culprits, whereupon we were quite rightly sternly punished.

During my third year at the school, I smuggled my faithful rifle back at the end of one holidays and kept it, dismantled in small pieces, in a false bottom which I built under my study desk. On Sundays, after chapel, I would leave the school gates dressed in walking-out uniform but carrying a bag containing the rifle and a change of clothes. Once out of sight of the school I would sneak into the forest reserve, quickly change clothes, hiding my uniform in a tree, assemble the rifle and set off towards Nairobi National Park about an hour and a half's walk away.

The journey was full of hazards; two major roads to cross, one by sprinting over when there was a gap in the traffic, the other by crawling underneath through a culvert. On one occasion the culvert was occupied by a warthog which fortunately was facing the other way, otherwise I might not be writing this now. The forest reserve was interlaced with vehicle tracks which were used by patrolling forest rangers; vehicle patrols were no problem because the noise always gave me sufficient warning to dive into the undergrowth, but foot patrols were often silent and usually able to spot a set of suddenly vanishing footprints.

If all went well, I could be in the park by midday and spend two hours exploring before having to start back. Strangely enough, despite my eagerness to hunt, I never shot anything in the park. The proximity of park headquarters also had something to do with this.

In any case, these expeditions came to a sudden end when one day's events proved to me that what I was doing was the height of stupidity. I heard rustlings, foot stamping and the breathing of what was obviously a very large animal. With heart pounding and puny rifle clutched at the ready I crawled through dense bush towards the noise. Eventually, peering through the leaves, I saw, at astonishingly close range, a huge female rhino with a calf. Almost at the same instant, the cow emitted a deafening snort and trotted forward, searching the wind for my scent.

I fled back a few yards to a large croton tree which I climbed with great alacrity. Pandemonium broke loose below me as both rhinos charged blindly past my tree puffing like steam engines, turned and charged back, noisily flattening the undergrowth below. At that point I felt a sharp, stinging bite on my leg and realised at once that I had disturbed a nest of fierce little black ants which were now crawling all over me. Now I had problems. The first was to physically stay in the tree – not an easy achievement when both hands were needed to slap ants. My second concern was for the precious rifle which, in my haste, I had left on the ground; the rhinos were trampling

WARTHOG FEEDING

dangerously close to it. However, my greatest worry was that all this noise would attract the attention of the rangers in which case I would be in serious trouble. After what seemed an age, during which time I had visited just about every ant-infested extremity of the tree, I reckoned the rhinos had moved sufficiently far away for me to descend and make a run for the boundary fence.

On my way back I was spotted by forest rangers who gave chase into dense bush but, having shaken them off, I realised I was lost. Only by climbing a tall tree could I find my bearings but the next hour was spent dodging patrols obviously alerted by my initial contact. The final drama in a thoroughly bad day was to be late for evening chapel and lose all privileges until the end of that term. So ended my National Park expeditions.

On the whole, despite these deviations, I was a law-abiding and reasonably diligent student. Art was my best subject and was taught by Professor Imberger, a short, rotund, elderly gentleman who, I believe, was a refugee from Nazi Germany. He spoke English with a very heavy accent and had absolutely no control over his teenage pupils who quickly learned the knack of reducing him to a state of apoplectic, speechless fury. I found it difficult in these circumstances to stand apart from my unruly peers and actually concentrate on the subject that I so enjoyed. However, I managed and the professor evidently thought I was worthy of more attention because he suggested I take extra tuition in my spare time.

The formal art syllabus, designed entirely for the final fourth form exams, gave little scope for originality, the only permitted medium being water-colours. In my extra hours, the professor taught me the basic principles of oil painting. I was intrigued at his ability to create a sky using his fingers, and the techniques he employed proved invaluable in later years. Thanks to his help, I added the art prize to my running and shooting trophies.

At seventeen I had had enough of school. I should have stayed an extra year and taken higher certificate examinations, but I persuaded my father to let me leave. I think I disappointed my parents who wanted me to go to art college in England, but exaggerated stories of the beatnik cult, which seemed most prevalent in that kind of establishment, were enough to put me off that plan completely. For some time I had entertained the idea of becoming a professional hunter; after all, I could shoot and felt I knew enough bushcraft and animal lore to qualify. There was too, the romantic image and promise of an exciting outdoor life. I kept these thoughts strictly to myself, my reticence perhaps prompted by an awareness that I had little or no experience with big game, elephant and lion in particular, which would have been a hunting client's main interest. I knew, also, that announcement of such intentions would have brought parental hysteria because it was a life filled with hazard and uncertainty. Instead, I decided to follow in Father's footsteps and farm. He tried to insist on the best grounding for such a career – an agricultural degree at a British university – but that was out of the question since my science grades were simply atrocious. In the end, I had my own way and found myself a job as a farm manager in Western Kenya.

At the time I was leaving school, Father was moving from my beloved Soysambu to a new farm at Kitale in Western Kenya. For me it was the end of an era, the end of a strange dual period of my life, love and hate; love for my homes at Solai and Soysambu which were everything a boy could ever wish for; hate for school, its lack of privacy, its regimentation, its discipline and dull routine. Of course, both were necessary to build character and self-reliance, but at the time nothing could have persuaded me that school should be included in the equation.

SAND RIVER STANDOFF

A buffalo will never run far before sliding to halt and turning to face the cause of his disturbance. I have tried to capture that moment of stillness when every muscle and nerve is taut with tension, every one of his senses strains to identify the intruder, his head is held high, the muzzle pointing menacingly, and the eyes seem to roll in their sockets exposing the whites. This is the animal's moment of decision. Attack or retreat? Whichever happens, he will give a long, hissing snort, toss his head and move with a speed and agility startling for an animal so heavy and apparently cumbersome.

CHEETAH REPOSE

These are truly the colours of Africa. I used only Crimson, Yellow Ochre, Burnt-Umber, Burnt Sienna and Cadmium Yellow. I never thin the paint because I feel to do so causes a "muddy" effect. The cheetah's coat is laid on with thick paint, the black (crimson and umber) spots separate from the light shade between; never one on top of the other. Then I work the paint with a blade-shaped brush, stroking it into a hair texture to conform to the actual lie of the animal's hair. The spots are merged into their light background, black hair overlaying light and vice versa depending on the direction of the coat's hair. Naturally, this process can only be done when the paint is wet. It sounds laborious but it suits my temperament. I enjoy it.

After helping my father move into his new farm at Kitale, I took a job as a farm manager some seventy miles away at an altitude of nine thousand feet up in the Highlands west of the Rift Valley. My boss was Denis Wetham, whose adventures before and during the war made my own seem positively insipid. He had a wicked sense of humour, the foulest of tempers until he had breakfasted, played a mean game of polo and was a master fly fisherman. A few years before my arrival one of his tractor drivers contracted TB so Denis retired him and taught him his own hobby – fly tying. Within a short time it was evident that he was a natural, producing high quality trout and salmon flies in surprisingly quick time.

By the time I was employed, there were three fly tyers and a thriving little business exporting their products as far away as Canada, Ireland and New Zealand. After the daily pre-dawn supervision of the milking it was my job to count, label and package the flies for their various destinations.

In my spare time I played mediocre rugby and tried to learn polo without any success. Denis had an intransigent pony named Fudge who resisted all attempts to be taught the game. In frustration, he virtually gave me the horse saying that we could damned well learn the game together. It was not long before Fudge and I reached mutual agreement that polo was not to be our *forte*. I had built up this relationship with some timidity, having been made to ride when I was seven, fallen quite badly, and vowed never to go near a horse again. However, that painful memory had faded and soon I was able to career around the farm at breakneck speed clinging to the stirrups with my bare toes – for some reason I could not ride wearing shoes – and waving a polo stick in the vain hope of persuading Fudge that we could still make a polo playing combination. The only time he took no notice of the polo stick was when I rode through the wheat and flushed an oribi (small antelope); then he would dash madly after it with little encouragement from me, quite oblivious of my wild yells and stick waving.

I had completely forgotten about painting. I think the only time I used a brush during those first years after school was to paint a magnificent rainbow trout which Denis caught in the Kaptagat forest. I was content with my job, enjoying both the work and social life, and had given no thought whatsoever to the long term future. I was taken aback, therefore, when one day Denis asked me if I intended spending the rest of my days as an underpaid farm manager. My first reaction was guarded wariness. Was this a subtle hint perhaps that I was not meeting up to expectations? However, living in the main house as part of the family I began to realise that Denis had a genuine concern for my future. I respected his wisdom and judgement and listened carefully to his reasoning, agreeing with the argument that I would simply vegetate in my current position. He insisted that I should get away from the ostrich-like existence in Kenya to broaden my experience so we set about investigating how that could be done bearing in mind that I had no training and no money. Little did I realise that these ideas and discussions presaged a major turning point in my life.

Denis found the answer: join the army. I was extremely dubious. The King's African Rifles (KAR) was a large force indigenous to the British possessions of East Africa. The rank and file were local Africans, whereas officers and senior NCOs were seconded from the British army. From the newspaper he unearthed a scheme to encourage local people to join as potential officers. Provided that the applicant successfully passed the various selection processes, he would spend two years at the Royal Military Academy, Sandhurst, followed by a mandatory three years with the colours. Five years did not seem too long, especially with the prospect of an all-expenses paid, two-year trip to England, so (with some misgivings based on the feeling that I would be returning to school) I applied.

CHEETAH STUDY

KILIMANJARO MORNING

Without any conscious intention, many of my recent works tend more towards a portrayal of Africa's environment and mood, than to the animals which live there. This painting is a prime example where I attempt to show the magnificent grandeur of Mt Kilimanjaro and how it dominates and dwarfs even the largest animals and trees. I often try to imagine the thoughts of the first explorers who struggled for miles across flat, waterless plains until one day they glimpsed Kilimanjaro's peak rising into the clouds like a phantom. What a moment.

Before any reply came, I received instructions to report for six months' compulsory military training – the draft. On the appointed day I reported to the training centre and within hours was questioning the wisdom of actually voluntering for this torture. After a month of purgatory suffered at the hands of a sergeant from the Brigade of Guards who must have qualified with honours at a school for sadists, my worst fears were realised: the sergeant found out that I was required to report to Nairobi for the first potential officer interview. He had a field day; so I wanted to be an officer, did I? My feet never touched the ground for the next twenty-four hours until, with huge relief, I fled through the camp gate to catch the Nairobi train.

Almost immediately the bottom fell out of my world – I failed the interview, and was ordered to resume my military training. I was totally stunned. I dreaded returning to the jibes of my fellow sufferers, and the mockery of the sergeant. He lived up fully to expectations, and I learnt further lessons in survival.

I was so incensed at having been rejected by the Nairobi board that I applied, as soon as I could, for the same interview the following year, determined that I should pass, and quite forgetting how thoroughly miserable I had been at the military training centre.

It was an eventful year's wait; my military training completed, I returned to Denis's farm for a few months but then, conscious of the fact that the interview would be followed (assuming I passed) by a compulsory, character-assessing climb of Mount Kilimanjaro, I decided to get fit and acclimatised. To that end I set off on my bicycle from our Kitale farm and headed for Mount Kenya, which I intended to climb. I never completed the 120-mile journey, succumbing instead to acute appendicitis and ending up in a small hospital having the offending organ removed.

I decided to convalesce at Lake Naivasha on a friend's farm which adjoined the lake. Along the shore he grew beautiful, lush green lucerne for his cattle. Unfortunately the lucerne fields were frequently invaded by an army of hippopotamuses which laid waste to his precious crop. To counter this offensive he employed night guards armed with thunderflashes and Greener guns (simple, single-barrelled shotguns loaded with buckshot) who managed to some extent to keep the giant munch-men at bay.

One night when I was there a guard fired his shotgun at almost point blank range at an invading hippo and, sure enough, next morning a trail of blood led off into the papyrus swamp which flanked the lake. Maybe the anaesthetic had affected my brain because I volunteered to look for it with a borrowed rifle. I was still at the stage where my stomach hurt if I laughed, so climbing through a papyrus swamp was the worst possible activity. One minute I would be up to my elbows in water, the next struggling onto the tangled mass of roots and stems that made up the papyrus island. If the hippo had decided to charge I would not have stood a chance. After an unsuccessful morning's search I decided there must be an easier method. I emerged from the swamp, covered in leeches, which we removed with hot cigarette ends. That afternoon I commandeered a punt and set off again with a local volunteer to find the wounded hippo.

It soon became apparent that my companion had no idea how to propel

HIPPO

LIONESS

This lioness could well have been placed in position by Central Casting. She was alone, which probably meant she had cubs. The evening sun spotlighted her pale coat against the dark-coloured rocks and bleached, dry grass softened the contrast and allowed a blending with her environment. Silhouetted against the sky she turned her head this way and that, ears pricked alertly, for all the world like a top professional model in front of our madly clicking cameras. It was the sort of scene which, at the end of a long hot day in the bush, brings a sigh of contentment at the perfection of it all.

THE RUBBING ROCK

An ancient boulder thrown onto the plains centuries ago by volcanic activity has a surface polished as smooth as glass. It is just the right height to attract the attention of all the larger mammal species, from antelopes to elephants. Countless animals have rubbed and scratched their sides on it, trying to dislodge their parasites and relieve their many itches. The hooves and feet of all its diverse visitors have worn a trench round its base. Elephants will plaster it with mud from their recent wallow. This will act as a grinding paste for subsequent attendants, each successive one adding lustre to the worn surface.

a punt so, instructing him to hold the rifle and hand it to me quickly if I yelled, I stood in the bows and poled out into the swamp. As we eased silently through the tangled waterlilies, jumping with fright as waterbirds fled startled by our approach, I spotted a hippo's head submerging in a large open space between papyrus islands. I stopped and was about to ask for the rifle when the water erupted just ahead and a huge gaping mouth looked as if it was about to engulf both ourselves and the boat. My assistant fell to the bottom of the punt still clutching the rifle, and lay on top of it obviously convinced that his end had come. I had some sympathy with that thought as I teetered precariously on the violently rocking boat wondering whether a punt pole would be sufficient deterrent if the hippo returned. Thankfully, it did not and I returned to shore quietly convincing myself that the wounded animal must have died. If it had not, someone else could seek it out and take responsibility for finishing it off.

At the other end of the farm, another pest was causing havoc – zebras. Hundreds of these animals regularly invaded, despite the existence of fences. Several zebras would lie on their sides, work their heads under the lowest strand of wire, scrabble with their feet and heave themselves forwards. Eventually, either the wire snapped or the nearest post broke as more and more animals joined the attack.

The only way to get rid of them at this stage seemed to be to shoot one or two and drive the remainder back across the boundary before repairing the fence yet again. However, zebras are highly intelligent animals and would only graze in the middle of the open plains where it was impossible to approach on foot to within an effective range. They would allow a vehicle within that range but as soon as it stopped, they galloped away in a cloud of dust. My answer to the problem was to fall out of the moving Land Rover on the blind side and lie motionless in the grass as the zebras watched the vehicle drive away. In this way, I managed to bag one, but in so doing burst half the stitches from my appendix scar.

I was therefore in fairly battered shape the following week when I reported to the long anticipated interview board in Nairobi for the second time. I am not sure whether it was my persistence which got me through or the hilarity I raised when asked discreetly why I was scratching. Some days after a leech has been removed, the place where it was attached will start to itch excruciatingly. Most of my leeches had latched on around my nether regions which were on fire as I exercised every atom of will power to resist scratching but eventually, to no avail. I removed a hand from under my backside and with a lop-sided grin of embarrassment, fiercely attacked the source of my discomfort.

I was nineteen years of age and the significance of my position now dawned on me. My whole life was about to change and I wondered if I had made the right decision. In any event, the last thought that entered my mind was anything remotely connected with art. As far as I was concerned, I had swapped from being a farmer to being a soldier.

At that time, the three East African territories of Kenya, Tanganyika and Uganda were still under British colonial rule. In order to prepare us newly recruited officer cadets for the rigours of the Royal Military Academy, Sandhurst, we were sent to the Uganda battalion of the KAR based in Jinja on the Nile where that great river flows out of Lake Victoria. We were a mixed bunch, some of us having already completed our compulsory military service, others with no idea of which end of a rifle was which. To avoid repetition, I was given another task whilst my compatriots learned to march up and down and stamp their feet. I was introduced to Idi Amin and told to teach him basic etiquette as required in an officers' mess and also that hooligan's game played by gentlemen, rugby. I have to admit I did a rather poor job on both counts. Amin then held the rank of Effendi, a colonial appointment somewhere between warrant officer and subaltern.

On the rugby field, provided that he could get hold of the ball, Idi was hard to stop since he could run strongly for a man of his size. I was teaching him to hand off a potential tackler, explaining carefully that an actual physical blow to the opponent was strictly forbidden. When I thought the lesson had penetrated, I told him to run towards me and hand me off when I moved in to tackle. The next thing I knew was waking into semi-consciousness, feeling as if I had been bludgeoned with a plank and looking into the large, concerned face of Idi who evidently could not understand the difference between a hand-off and a karate chop.

One night we were required to take part in a night navigation exercise. Idi and I were duly paired off with instructions to cover a five-mile course through the hills near the shores of the lake. There was sufficient light from the stars to make it a relatively easy task and one of my bearings pointed us between two prominent trees on the slope below. I set off ahead but was brought to a violent and nightmarish halt when I reached the two trees and realised too late that between them was a massive bird spiders' web. An adult bird spider can measure six inches from leg tip to leg tip. The legs and thorax of these spiders are thin and shiny black, the abdomen an obscene white blob, and they bite. I inherited a spider phobia from my mother and never was it more manifest than with bird spiders. Imagine, therefore, my horror to feel these foul creatures all over me as I flailed around in the dark anticipating their evil fangs sinking into my face at any moment. Finally, I broke free and collapsed drained and shaking in the grass to find that Idi seemed equally incapacitated, only in his case it was with laughter.

Many other strange and incongruous events happened in Jinja but their place is not in this book. Sandhurst was my next stop, apart from a one-month stay at the British Army's education establishment at Beaconsfield, where we "foreigners" were required to read the newspapers every day to improve our English.

For the next two years I stayed at the military academy, keeping my nose reasonably clean and gaining only a brief moment of notoriety when I competed in a race over one mile in early winter on a cinders track, barefooted. My only excursions into art were endless caricatures of our various tutors, and designing and painting the scenery for the academy's rendition of the Mikado. I missed Kenya desperately and counted the days for the course to end. At last it did, and in August 1962 I graduated as a second lieutenant in the King's African Rifles.

Frustratingly, I was kept on in England to attend an arms course in Kent, followed by a platoon commanders' course on the Salisbury Plain which started in January 1963, during the most severe winter for many years. The depth of snow on the Plain was such that the normal course programme was impossible to follow so, as an officer in a tropical army, I was taught to make igloos, snow shoes and skis and how to survive in Arctic conditions by one of the hardest men I have ever met, an officer in the Special Boat Service. I contributed my own collection of tropical traps to his repertoire, and we got on famously.

Finally it was time to go home, and what a relief it was to be back in Kenya. Politically, much had changed in my absence. Independence, from being a reluctantly discussed possibility, had become an inevitability; in fact a date had been set for it to happen later that year. I was asked if I would like to transfer to the British Army, to which I quickly declined, still having the intention of quitting once my three years were up.

REFLECTION

Cape buffaloes congregate in large herds comprised mainly of females and young with a few dominant bulls in attendance. The remaining males will form their own small herds and live some distance from the main group. Most members of these bachelor groups are old, battle-scarred and bad-tempered rejects. The hair has been worn from their hides and their massive horns meet in the centre of their heads in a great, ridged, armoured boss. Their gait is deceptively ponderous, looking for all the world like that of an arthritic old man, but that illusion will be quickly dispelled if danger threatens.

In the clear, early morning light they graze contentedly, never far from water if possible. By mid-morning, when the sun begins to burn, they will quench their thirst at the nearest water and search for a suitable wallow in which to lie up during the heat of the day.

HUNTING DOGS

These African hunting dogs (their zoological name translated means spotted wolf) stand on the bank of the Tiva River, which, for most of the year, is a flat, dry expanse of sand dotted with holes where the elephants have dug for the water which lies just a few feet below the surface. The surrounding countryside, at first glance, appears uncompromisingly inhospitable, the heat is searing and each piece of sparse vegetation seems to sprout needle-sharp thorns of every shape and size. Yet, surprisingly, animals and birds are in abundance. I have often wondered whether they live here out of preference or whether, over the years, pressure from man has forced them to move into ever harsher environments.

The colours here are really evocative, to me typical of everything wild and dramatic about Africa. Red earth, silvery-grey scrub, sun-bleached grass and black rocks all combine to make a perfect colour setting for any animal. The black, yellow and white dogs blend particularly well.

The baobab tree in the background, probably many hundreds of years old, accentuates the impression of heat and dryness with its aged silver bark and leafless branches.

Across the border, Uganda was already independent and, further west, the Congo was in turmoil. The day I walked out of Sandhurst I was approached by a total stranger who seemed to know I was from Africa and invited me to join a mercenary force in the Congo. I declined but a close friend chose that option instead of the Parachute Regiment. Less than a year later I met him in Kenya destitute, desperate and lucky to be alive.

I joined 3 KAR stationed near Nairobi and almost immediately was given charge of the battalion shooting team, sent to a remote area west of Mount Kenya and told to come back only when we were all fit and sharp enough to win the Kenya Trophy. This was an annual march-and-shoot event competed for with great intensity by all the KAR battalions as well as units of the British Army. It was the kind of brief which was really up my street and I spent an idyllic three months "in the wilderness" moulding my team, free from the petty dictates of authority.

I remember one incident in particular from that excursion. One evening I was about two miles from camp hunting for the pot when, to my astonishment, I saw a wild dog trotting towards me through the *leleshwa* scrub. Soon I realised that there was a substantial pack all around me, showing no signs of fear. I had never seen a wild dog, but had heard many gruesome stories about their ruthlessness and ability to take on anything. With that in mind I sidled carefully towards the nearest tree, rifle ready, wondering how true was the theory that if I shot one, the others would devour it, thus giving me time to climb the tree. As it was, they circled around me showing only curiosity before disappearing silently into the dark. In view of my ignorance of these extraordinary animals which, in those days, were subject to more inaccurate legend than any other species, it was an unnerving experience.

Later that year we won the Kenya trophy, which did my reputation no harm and earned me promotion to full lieutenant. December was the month when full independence would be granted and preparations started long in advance for this memorable ceremonial occasion. Most men from the Kenya KAR battalions would take part, but it was decided that any under 5 feet 10 inches would lessen the impressiveness of the display. It would also be inappropriate if a white junior officer (and I was the only one) were to be included. A month or so before the great event, trouble broke out in north-eastern Kenya in a 65,000-square mile area populated by Somali tribesmen who wanted to secede their traditional homeland from Kenya and join Somalia itself. Opportunist attacks had been made on several remote police stations, so the authorities decided that a show of force was needed.

With most of the army committed to the independence parade a small force of "cooks and bottlewashers", all under 5 foot 10 inches, was sent to the north-eastern province to show the flag. I went too, and gladly, since I disliked anything ceremonial. We established camp in some abandoned school buildings on the outskirts of Garissa, made ourselves comfortable and looked forward to a life of gentle leisure for the next few weeks. It was therefore a rude surprise when our camp was attacked by *shifta* – a name for a bandit – that very first night. Although the attack was made from a great distance by a hopelessly inexperienced gang of shiftas who fled into the bush after the first few shots, the chaos it caused was indescribable.

I recall the brief look of incredulity on the face of my commander before we simultaneously doused the light and fumbled around in the dark to find our respective weapons. Away in the main school our soldiers were equally disorganised, firing randomly in all directions until finally they were brought under control. When the dust had settled and a roll call had been made, it was discovered that two men were wounded, by our own side.

I relate this incident because, in a roundabout way, it was another turning

SAMBURU GERENUK

Face on, the gerenuk is truly an extraordinary shape, especially its tiny head perched ridiculously on top of such a long neck. The head itself appears quite out of proportion to the ears and horns, and the face seems to be made up almost entirely of nose.

This painting shows the animal standing in the minimal shade of a small species of acacia peculiar to the harsh environment in which it lives. It feeds from the sparse leaves of this tree, delicately plucking them from between an array of needle-sharp thorns. Gerenuks need never drink, gaining all the moisture they require from these same leaves.

point in my life, helping me on my way to becoming a painter. The incident proved to the authorities that the problem in the north-east was not just a matter of a handful of hotheaded dissidents, but the start of a substantial commitment by the military to a mean and dirty guerilla war which was to last for the next four years. I was there on and off from the start and became more involved than most in a sordid drama which produced short spells of violent action between long spells of boredom. It was the boredom which finally drove me to look for a means of passing the time.

And so I started to draw.

This phenomenon was, however, a gradual one. In the early stages I was commanding a platoon, which gave me little leisure. We were deployed in a region that was completely different from anything I had previously experienced. North-eastern Kenya has a harsh climate of high temperatures and strong winds. The terrain is semi-desert, supporting mile upon flat mile of the unmerciful "wait-a-bit" thorn. We would encounter sudden ranges of stark, rocky hills, high mountains and unexpected waterholes surrounded by dense acacia groves. There were spectacular colours: rocks ranging from ochre to deep red; blinding white, sandy soil; and always the grey, mauve and purple scrub. Game was plentiful – elephants, giraffes, lions, Grevy zebras, oryx, long-necked gerenuks, warthogs, dikdiks and hundreds of different species of birds. It was wild and raw and wonderful.

At the end of 1963, early in the affair, we were assigned to Moyale, an outpost situated astride the Kenya/Ethiopia border. Soon after our company's arrival I was ordered to a location some seventy miles due south where it was suspected the shifta gangs may be infiltrating eastwards out of the Somali homeland. With thirty-five men I travelled for a day following cattle tracks and game trails. We arrived in a place where there was no sign of human habitation, and where, evidently, no-one had passed through for a long time. My orders were to remain there a month, which suited me very well because I had seldom seen a more perfect situation. To the west was a fifty- or sixty-foot high wall of black lava which ran for miles in a north-south direction, the result of a comparatively recent volcanic eruption. On the rare occasions when it rained, the water filtered through the porous lava and came out along the eastern side of the ridge, where it collected in a series of deep pools. We established base at one such pool where the water was crystal clear to a depth of fifteen feet. At the end of our month most of the soldiers had learnt to swim. I hunted oryx and guinea fowl to interrupt the monotony of corned beef. Some miles to the south I found an extensive swamp which seethed with waterbirds, including great numbers of winter migrants. This was paradise and I never wanted to leave.

However, it had to end, and we returned to Moyale to hear disturbing news that elements of the armies in Tanzania and Uganda had mutinied and that even one of the Kenya battalions was having trouble. The company was assembled and given a no-nonsense lecture on the subject by our British Army company commander. It was evident to me that this far from pleased the men, who seemed to feel that they were virtually being accused without having committed the deed. Later, as one of the platoons was allowed the afternoon off to visit the town, my own men stayed in camp and surreptitiously called me aside to discuss the matter. In essence they were warning me that all hell could break loose, that *I* was in no danger, but that the other two white officers had better watch out. I warned them of what I had heard.

The Kenyan part of Moyale was a Muslim community where alcohol was forbidden. By contrast the Ethiopian side was a rabbit warren of brothels and beer halls selling particularly potent liquor. That afternoon the off-duty platoon found their way across the border and within hours were tanked up and in a collectively ugly mood. When only a few had staggered back to camp by check-in time, I was dispatched with some of my own men to find the remainder. Hours of coaxing and sometimes non-too-gentle cajoling finally prised the last of them from Mama Kilele's (Madam Noisey's), the most notorious bordello in town where, incidentally, it was possible to buy Maria Theresa taler coins for a few Kenya shillings.

As we approached camp with the stragglers, there was pandemonium. Several men had broken into the armoury, snatched up their rifles, fixed bayonets and were racing around the camp in a thoroughly menacing fashion. Luckily, they had not reached the ammunition store, otherwise there could have been a disaster, but it was still a very frightening experience. One soldier charged towards me bellowing like a bull, bayonet pointing at my midriff. I have no idea what went through my mind in those split seconds – probably nothing because I stood still like a rabbit in shock. He stopped as if to clear his head, and wheeled away to look for someone else.

In such a situation it could have been fatal to adopt a tough approach; besides, I was much too scared. My commander was nowhere to be found, and so for the next few hours by extra-gentle persuasion I tried with some success to identify and isolate the worst offenders, and quietly suggest they cool down. I signalled headquarters in Nairobi and asked for help, which arrived by air the next day in the person of the first African to reach the position of company commander. Later he went on to command the entire armed forces of Kenya.

S omalis are a tough, uncompromising people so for this reason it was sometimes deemed necessary to employ equally ruthless tactics. We were ordered to a remote waterhole, where the shifta attacks had been particularly prevalent. We were to stake out the area and confiscate all stock which came to drink. This was a particularly effective method of bringing the local people to their knees: all their animals had to come to that water every day, and we were instantly depriving one community after another of its entire livelihood. By the end of one day we had collected about nine thousand head of camels and cattle. It was a strange day of humour and pathos, chaos and tension, noise, dust, heat and flies. In a normal day each family would bring their animals to drink at different times carefully arranged to avoid mixing the herds. Our intervention brought anarchy; cattle and camels from different herds were mingling, fighting, mating and, above all bawling their heads off in hunger and confusion. Over this whole scene hung a great pall of dust and away on the

GABBRA GIRL WITH CAMEL

CAMEL HERD

I cheated a bit in this painting, which depicts the desert area adjoining Lake Turkana in the north of Kenya. The herdsboy is a Samburu, ethnically and linguistically close to the Masai. Although their traditional homelands reach close to Lake Turkana, the Samburu are more cattle people than keepers of camels. However, I decided to stretch the technicalities because the young man's dress, posture and aloneness seemed so appropriate to the stark surroundings and drab, dusty dryness of the camel herd. They lead a harsh life in an inhospitable environment where the danger of raids by neighbouring nomadic tribes is ever present.

ALERT

The background to this painting is similar to many of my works where I want to achieve maximum emphasis on the main subject in the foreground. At the same time, I try to give an impression of depth and distance by using the shapes and colours of the subject's actual environ-ment. The same effect is acquired by looking through almost closed eyes or from an out-of-focus telephoto lens. To create this effect, I paint the background in some detail; then, whilst the paint is still wet, stroke it boldly in one direction with the largest brush in my collection. This produces a blur, dissolves all detail and gives an impressionistic effect and low-key background for a strong foreground subject.

fringes the owners of the herds squatted resignedly in what little shade was available, resenting and hating us for what we were doing. The next morning we started to drive this great herd the sixty-odd miles to the nearest army base at Wajir.

That march is stamped indelibly on my mind. The heat was crucifying and the dust raised by thousands of hooves was choking. There was only one watering point on the way, and many animals were abandoned to die of thirst. We stopped for the first night and corralled the stock inside a makeshift wait-a-bit thorn *zariba* (enclosure). The noise of hungry, thirsty animals was deafening. As dusk fell we selected a steer and slaughtered it to feed the men, but as one huge Masai soldier was holding a lantern aloft to give light to the butchering, shots rang out from the other side of the herd and I could hear the angry hiss of bullets uncomfortably close.

My first reaction was to hurl myself at Lemisoi, the Masai, to get rid of the light. We flattened ourselves to the ground as firing intensified beyond the herd and flares lit up the sky. This was too much for the cattle and they stampeded, demolishing the flimsy *zariba*, and headed directly for our position. Hobson's choice: stand up to be shot or stay down to be trampled. I must have chosen the former because I soon found myself frantically treading backwards, trying to stay on my feet as the leading animals came towards me. Luckily, as they reached darkness and thick bush they lost momentum and I was able to disentangle myself, painfully and shakily, from a thorn bush, and begin trying to restore order. Shots and flares were still being fired, soldiers were shouting and running in all directions trying to locate their belongings or round up the cattle and camels, officers were bellowing orders and the shifta, or what was left of them, were heading for the horizon as fast as they could run. It transpired that a small force had crept up under cover of darkness, obviously bent on retribution, and opened fire at close range. Miraculously, we only had one man wounded but the shifta suffered heavy casualties.

When order had been restored, the British major in charge of the operation summoned his subalterns for a debriefing. As he handed out a slug of whisky to each of us he leaned close to me and in a low, fatherly voice asked if it was my first time under fire. I was comforted to see the bottle in his hand rattling against the glass like a machine gun. I was not the only one to have been scared out of his wits. The stock was rounded up, the zariba repaired and we waited out the remainder of a very jittery night without much sleep. Well before dawn we were on our way again, forcing those poor animals forward at a punishing pace, trying to reach Wajir before the searing sun took its toll. Being the only white face patrolling the flanks in thick thorn bush, I felt extremely vulnerable and cannot think of another occasion when my adrenalin was driving my pulse so hard for such an extended period of time.

That operation forced me to ponder for the first time the stupidity and cruelty of war, even though this was not one in the true sense of the word. We must have caused so much pain and suffering in just three days, yet how else could such a situation be controlled other than by punishing the people who supported the enemy?

M y six action-packed months commanding a platoon in the field came to an abrupt and welcome end when I was promoted to captain and appointed intelligence officer, with a comfortable office at field headquarters in Garissa and the chance to indulge in a favourite pastime – the study of maps, which I stuck to every available wall space and covered with a multitude of coloured pins. I was also appointed messing officer responsible for the officers' food, much of which was wild game that I hunted in the surrounding bush.

A QUAIL QUAILS

How many times does one wish that certain split-second moments in time could be frozen for posterity? The great privilege of a painter or photographer is to be able to achieve that and many of my paintings strive towards that end.

Here is an example. A serval cat poised motionless, straining every one of its senses to pinpoint the quail which crouches under the tussock of grass. The quail has three options – run, fly or freeze. Natural instinct will dictate which to choose but any of them are fraught with danger. The cat also expects any of the three and readies itself to react accordingly – chase, swipe or pounce.

The trick is to set the scene for potential action and leave the viewer to speculate on the outcome.

THREAT DISPLAY

The bush and trees beside the track were thick and impenetrable. I caught a glimpse of movement behind the tangle and stopped the car. Suddenly, with great crashings and trumpeting, I saw an elephant through the tangled mass, charging with great determination. I raised the camera and pressed the button, gunned the engine and beat a hasty retreat.

The photograph showed only details of one eye, part of an ear and a piece of the trunk but the memory was vivid. I was able to peel back the undergrowth and piece together the hitherto concealed parts of the elephant.

Early one morning I was hunting the beautiful vulturine guinea fowl which ran in large flocks along the banks of the Tana River. They fly with great reluctance but run for ever, and provided they are cooked for about a week, are excellent eating. I paused to water Africa, and had reached full flow when I glanced casually upwards to stare with considerable alarm into the eyes of a very large elephant which was standing motionless behind a thin screen of branches. Several minor accidents took place below waist level as I endeavoured to tiptoe quietly backwards. It seemed that the elephant waited in a gentlemanly fashion for me to get through and button up before letting rip with a multi-decibel trumpet and erupting half way out of the bush in a cloud of dust and splintered wood. I turned tail and fled but he didn't follow. I'm sure I heard him chuckling as I beat the untidiest of retreats. I was lucky because the Tana River elephants at that time were mean and aggressive. Unaccustomed to the hunter's guns or arrows, they still regarded man as an impudent intruder and often would not hesitate to see him off.

In the heat of the day, Garissa, like most other parts of northern Kenya, is a flat, dreary, shimmering place where the heat saps one's energy and the dry wind blows tiringly and monotonously. The only consolation is the Tana River, flanked by tall, cool trees and fresh, green undergrowth, as it flows sluggishly past the town. However, for a few hours after sunrise the countryside is alive with birdsong and animals taking advantage of dawn's coolness before the heat clamps down once more. This was my time to replenish the officer's larder, before I was expected in the office.

In my new appointment I worked closely with police special branch and in particular with a mad Irishman, formerly a member of the Royal Ulster Constabulary. Paddy (that, indeed, was his name) invited me on several occasions to join him in hairbrained schemes to make contact with shifta gangs. He had accumulated his own force of Somalis – so-called defectors who he reckoned had a grudge against the guerilla movement. He had organised the construction of an armoured truck camouflaged as a trader's lorry. To outward appearances it looked just that, with a load of four-gallon tins of ghee, but behind the first row of tins was an open-roofed box made of half-inch armour containing eight men armed to the teeth. In temperatures often exceeding 100°F we travelled many miles over appalling roads cooking like turkeys in this awful contraption and hoping that a shifta gang would be gullible enough to stop it. The idea then was for the driver to wait until they were within range before ducking into his own armoured cab and ringing a bell in the back which would prompt us to leap up and do battle. It never worked – I am sure Paddy's "defectors" had warned every shifta within a hundred miles!

Another idea was to patrol deep into bandit territory disguised as shiftas in the hope that we would be mistaken for another gang. This too proved fruitless, although we had some interesting contacts with wildlife. One night we were sleeping in the bush when a herd of elephants blundered into the camp. The sentry panicked and opened up at close range with his bren gun. Nothing can wake you up faster, and cause more consternation, than a burst of gunfire at close range. I thought we were being

ELEPHANT STUDY

PROTECTING THE FLANKS

There is a conflict in this painting between authenticity and artistic licence. I wanted a dramatic scene filling the long canvas with running elephants and dust as a background to the angry guardians of the herd. In normal times the mature cows would perform this task since elephants maintain a matriarchal society. However, I decided to surrender to the romantic notion of the herd bulls protecting their lumbering family.

In present reality, my portrayal is actually, sadly true. In times of great stress, the bachelor bulls and the small matriarchal groups will join together in large herds for mutual security. These are indeed times of stress when man is killing elephants daily. Therefore, I feel some guilt in painting a true scene of harrassment when the cause of the painting's authenticity is the greedy immorality of my fellow human beings.

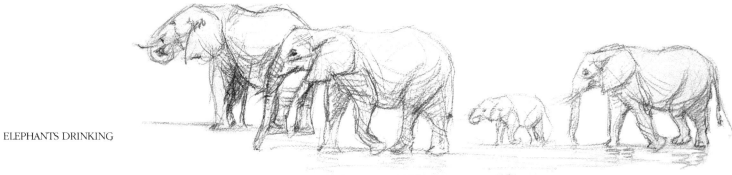

ELEPHANTS DRINKING

attacked and was still fumbling with my sub-machine gun when I heard the elephants trumpeting and realised what had happened. It was a brilliant moonlit night, so bright that the elephant tracks and spots of blood were clearly visible. Hurriedly, we strapped on equipment and followed the trail, but never again caught up with the herd despite tracking them for the rest of the night. I had read stories about elephants supporting a wounded colleague and actually saw evidence of it that night. It was obvious from the tracks that the wounded animal was flanked by two others, but as daylight broke there was less and less blood and the wounded one seemed to be moving independently. Reluctantly, we gave up the chase and never found out how bad its injuries had been. I hoped, perhaps naively, that it would survive.

Apart from such incidents and the occasional shifta contact somewhere out in the province, life at Garissa revolved round the local club, where one drank copious quantities of beer or drove out into the bush to shoot. Hunting was beginning to pall and the club activities were hard on my meagre earnings, so I resolved to find a new interest. Although, since school, I had done no serious art, I was forever doodling, particularly in lectures and meetings, when I would draw caricatures of others in the room. This time I made a conscious effort and started to draw and sketch the local tribesmen around the base. It was enjoyable and kept me out of most mischief, and my fellow officers' critical acclaim eventually prompted me to take the portfolio to Nairobi when I next had some leave.

After Garissa's monastic existence, leave in Nairobi comprised a frantic scramble to attend as many parties as possible. At one of these I met a girl who painted horses and dogs. My attention came sharply into focus when she explained that a professional hunter friend had an American client who was interested in acquiring two paintings of a Masai man and woman. I gathered that she was reluctant to take on the order so, in a rash moment and on the strength of her enthusiasm over my drawings, I said I would try it myself. Accordingly, I invested in a box of oil paints, two canvasses and two picture postcards of Masai. The resultant two paintings were approved by the American and I was paid the staggering sum of £50 each. This indeed, was food for thought. I had earned almost a month's salary in ten days.

I went back to Garissa flushed with success and determined to paint more, but this plan was immediately suspended when the battalion second-in-command, a major from the Parachute Regiment, cornered me over drinks and explained that there were plans to form a new airborne unit in the army. Since I was physically fit, the ideal size and had the right temperament (whatever that is) would I be interested? Of course, says I, senses numbed by the beer. Next morning he reminded me of my commitment and in a very short time I was back in Nairobi, enduring an agonising week of physical abuse to determine whether indeed I was suitable material to be a parachutist. Evidently I was, and soon learned that I was to be based at the Parachute School in England, where I would not only be trained myself but stay on to interpret instructions into Swahili for successive courses of black Kenyans. All thought of painting vanished in the excitement of this project.

My nine months at the Parachute School at Abingdon were filled with fun and humour. The Kenyans, most of whom had never flown, adapted quickly to parachuting although their techniques were often unorthodox. Thanks to their toughness there were few injuries and once the first man had jumped none of the others would dare lose face by refusing. The first descent was always a riot. Each man was supposed to land, unfasten his harness and run to report to the instructor in charge. More often than not, their astonishment

RESTLESS BEFORE THE STORM

As the storm clouds build over the Mara, humidity increases and the air is still. It is as if every living thing is holding its breath as it waits expectantly for the end of the dry season. Then a slight breeze ruffles the tips of the grasses and thunder rumbles in the distance. As the storms advance and hot air is replaced by cool, the wind strengthens and animals begin to fidget restlessly. Those which have been resting in the shade come to life as the temperature drops. Grass eaters display excitement at the prospect of more plentiful times. Carnivores emerge from cover hoping to exploit their prey's temporary preoccupation. The first big drops of rain hit the dry ground raising dust, soon followed by the deluge and everything that had started to move once more comes to a standstill to wait out the storm.

and delight at reaching *terra firma* in one piece prompted a display of yelling and dancing which would have put the most demonstrative goal scorer in the football league to shame. On cold winter days in the huge training hangar they would start spontaneous tribal singing and dancing to keep warm, bringing the entire establishment to a standstill.

At the end of each course the last descent was always done at night. This caused great consternation in my first group and endless questions about where they were going to land. On the appointed night I was waiting on the ground to bellow my Swahili instructions through a bull horn. The aircraft flew over and the blossoming parachutes could be seen against the night sky. Suddenly, a host of little lights appeared. Not to be fooled, each man had carried a flashlight and at eight hundred feet from the ground was eagerly pointing it downwards to see where he was going. The chief instructor staggered away speechlessly, shaking his head.

When each course had qualified, I took them to London, firstly to see the Tower which they thought was pretty tame stuff, and then on a mini-tour which included travelling by underground, for them the high point. We would spend an hour going up one escalator and coming down the other side, much to the astonishment of normal travellers, who must have thought we were all mad.

Not far down the road from the Parachute School I discovered an old pub which was run by six or seven beautiful girls. Susie was the one I fancied, and most of my evenings were spent there guzzling the free pints and prime steaks which she surreptitiously sneaked through the back door. Of course, that was not all we did and when I returned to Kenya she promised to follow, and so she did. We were married a year and a half later.

Shortly after returning to Kenya, I was promoted to major and given command of the new airborne unit, a post which I held for the next five years. In most respects it was a young officer's dream. I was answerable only to the army commander and since he knew nothing about parachuting, I could write my own training manual. I emphasised that we should train in wild and unpopulated areas, so a great deal of time was spent in the lesser-known game reserves. Under my command I had a remarkable group of men with whom, in the airborne tradition, I developed strong friendship and camaraderie, especially since I had seen each one of them through his trip to England and first parachute training. By virtue of the initial selection, they were the toughest the army could produce and rightly, if sometimes a little excessively, proud of it. I still count on most of them as close personal friends.

Much of the time was still spent in the north-eastern province, where we were employed from time to time as a special task force against the shifta. I had developed a strong affinity for this harsh landscape and relished my return there although after we were married, Susie was none too happy at the prospect of her new man being shot at. We never parachuted there, thank goodness – the wait-a-bit-thorn would have torn us to shreds and the wind was normally far too strong.

In other parts of Kenya I arranged training exercises designed for our proper role, and some of these brought interesting experiences.

At 5.30 one morning we took off from Nakuru airfield with three Caribou aircraft and headed east across the Rift Valley towards the open plains between the extinct volcanoes of Longonot and Suswa. This was to be simply a routine training jump, descending at dawn and marching twenty miles to an imaginary objective. I stood in the door of the aircraft, laden with weapon, ammunition, rations and equipment, longing to get out and relieve the discomfort. Over the drop zone the red light came on followed by the green and a dispatcher's thump on the shoulder with the shouted command, "Go". I walked off the sill and fell into space, buffeted momentarily by the slip stream, before looking up

CALLING THE CUBS

The lioness was lying alone on a rocky ridge staring intently at the plain below. Following her gaze I spotted a pair of warthogs running apparently aimlessly towards us. Suddenly she moved, snaking her way downwards, taking advantage of every piece of cover until she reached the long grass below. Her eyes never left the warthogs, monitoring their every move; when they stopped, so did she; when they moved, she angled towards their likely route. Thirty yards from her they sensed the danger, stopped short for a second and then bolted. She leapt from cover and gave chase, but the lead was too great and she soon gave up.

She climbed back up the ridge and I followed at a discreet distance. Her solitariness and swollen teats told me she had cubs. She paused, standing on a rock with her head raised as if to sniff the air. Then she uttered a soft, low, moaning sound and three small cubs tumbled out of a thicket to greet her exuberantly, each trying to outlick the other in an expression of joy at the reunion.

THE MIRAGE

At midday, on the floor of Kenya's Rift Valley, the heat reflects fiercely off the ground creating a shimmering, eye-dazzling mirage. Distant hills give the illusion of being immersed in a lake and animals' shapes distort and wobble in the turbulence.

I approached the subject with some apprehension and shied away from overdoing the effect. Similar to an incredible sunset, I felt the viewer might be disbelieving if I painted the mirage as I actually saw it.

To add a certain tension to the scene, I decided to portray giraffes and zebras galloping through the heat. I think the effect of urgent movement was remarkably increased by the addition of puffs of dust where the giraffes' hooves had hit the ground moments before.

to see the welcome canopy billowing above. The eastern horizon was red with the rising sun, whilst below the land was just acquiring definition as darkness disappeared.

In the routine way I released the heavy bundle of equipment that had been strapped to my harness and watched as it fell to dangle below me on the end of a rope. Then I started to take stock of the drop zone itself, and away in the distance could just discern my safety party. Below me, however, something was moving and I soon realised that it was a large herd of giraffes. As I kept on descending they seemed totally unaware that ninety men were about to land in their midst. Only when my bundle of equipment flashed past the nose of a big bull quickly followed by a pair of boots and me, did he pull up short, rocking back on his powerful hind legs. I was glad I landed in front and not behind, and wondered what chaos was about to ensue.

Either giraffes cannot look up or they thought we were a flock of huge birds, but none of them reacted until the first of us landed in their midst and stood up. It must have been a terrible shock and they certainly reacted violently, stampeding away in all directions. It was a miracle that no-one either landed astride a giraffe, which would have had interesting consequences, or was trampled. Some of the giraffes actually had their feet tangled in the canopies and rigging lines, but fortunately managed to free themselves.

Later, as we gathered on a nearby road, a vehicle pulled up with a local professional hunter and his clients who had just finished a safari. My hand was pumped by an American who swore enthusiastically that he had never seen the likes and would dine out on the experience for the rest of his life. Hot-di-gi-di!

W e also trained at the coast, enjoying parachuting at zero altitude, where the rate of descent was noticeably slower than up-country at 6,000 feet above sea level. Once we were asked to demonstrate our capabilities to the President, Jomo Kenyatta, so accordingly I selected a drop zone on an airstrip close to the sea just north of Mombasa. I jumped first and looked down to see a cluster of people and large limousines, but was disconcerted to realise that I was probably going to miss the drop zone. Indeed, that did happen. I plummeted through the branches of a huge baobab tree, crossing my legs and praying a bit, and stopped with a jerk just two feet from the ground. As I hung there, two heavily armed and camou-flaged men from the police general service unit leaped to their feet and threw their hands in the air. These were part of the "enemy" force which we were to "attack". I struggled out of my harness and marched off with my "pri-soners" to find the rest of my men.

It transpired that I was the only one to miss the drop zone and later, as we were introduced to the President, he chuckled and told me quietly in Swahili that there was no discrimination in Kenya.

We moved north beyond Malindi and did a practice jump on some salt flats. Because we would be flying over the sea, I had carefully explained to all the soldiers the need to wear life

GIRAFFE STUDY

THE VANTAGE POINT

Less than a hundred years ago, this rocky ridge overlooking the Mara River was covered in trees. Every year the Masai tribesmen burn the grasslands before the onset of the rains and these fires eventually destroy the trees aided, to some extent, by elephants. All that remain now are the skeletons but new, vigorous grass has grown through attracting a different group of animals.

Each dead tree attracts termites which build their mounds surrounding the source of their sustenance. In turn, these provide food for the antbear who burrows through the concrete-hard exterior with its powerful claws to the heart of the colony. The termites leave and the gaping hole becomes home to mongooses, snakes, a monitor lizard or even nesting birds. The mound itself is used by predators as a lookout and by elephants as a scratching point. And so it goes on.

MARA PLAINS

Sometimes, a visitor to Africa will look back on his safari and recall one place or one moment when all the ingredients for perfection seemed to be there. Often I am asked to recreate such memories on canvas. I find the task difficult, if not impossible; no two people think alike and one's own idea of paradise might seem indifferent to someone else.

This scene was described to me with eloquent enthusiasm. A tent pitched on the shore of a small lake fringed with water lilies, home to a pair of hippos and a host of water birds; fish eagles crying in the tall trees; elephants drinking; monkeys and baboons providing endless interest and amusement; lions roaring at night. But it was the view beyond the lake which captured the imagination; thousands of wildebeest mingled with zebras, gazelles and giraffe on the dry yellow grass plain which swept away to the distant wall of the Soit Ololol escarpment.

This time the task was easy. I too had camped there and fully endorsed all his superlatives.

jackets. They were shown in detail how to operate them in, the event of landing in water and it was particularly emphasised that *first* you had to release the harness and *then* inflate the jacket. As we descended I noticed that the salt flats were covered with water – the tide was in, and the depth of water was two inches at the most. However, this caused consternation in the sky behind me and several men forgot all they had been told and pulled the life jacket inflation tag, no doubt convinced that they were heading for the bottom of the ocean. The effect was comical. The life jacket bulged out between the parachute harness straps, forcing the wearer's arms to shoot out sideways and take no further part in the proceedings. They landed like rubber balls and lay there like stranded whales until someone could release their harnesses.

We made camp that evening in the forest near Malindi. I was lying on my camp bed reading, still fully clothed with my feet on the ground when a junior officer outside the tent shouted with considerable urgency "Keep still, sir!" I heard a dry, rustling sound and glancing from the corner of my eye, saw an enormous, dark-coloured snake heading straight towards me very fast, its head and two or three feet of its body off the ground and its mouth wide open. I froze and in an instant it had passed over my legs, ducked under the low canvas bed, come out the other side and hidden itself behind my suitcase which was a few feet away.

Like something from a Tom and Jerry cartoon, I erupted first vertically and then horizontally out of the tent, seemingly without touching the ground. I screamed for a gun and was soon handed one. Cocking it, I crept cautiously back inside, peeped behind the suitcase, identified the snake's head, aimed and fired. After a suitable wait I peeped carefully again and saw that my shot had killed it. We pulled it out, eight feet and two inches of black mamba. Then we saw the cause of its strange behaviour. Two or three inches were missing from the end of its tail and the raw stump was covered with a mass of safari ants. A minute later I started to shake and made serious inroads into a whisky bottle. One bite from that monster could have been fatal.

O ne of the last manoeuvres I planned took place in the Masai Mara. We parachuted into Narok airfield with 150 men and then marched for two days to the Mara river across wild country which is now mile after mile of wheat. We crossed the river on the third day and moved across the Mara triangle through a vast herd of buffalo. In a patch of forest where Kichwa Tembo lodge now stands we were charged by a rhino. Soldiers scattered, laughing and cursing, in all directions but when I fired several shots in the air the rhino veered off and fled. There are four lodges in that area now, hordes of tourist buses and no rhino.

To the west of the Mara River is a 1,500-foot-high escarpment which we climbed close to where it reaches the Tanzania border. We reached the top near a small village that belonged to an enclave of the Kipsigis tribe. They must have thought we were invaders because they fled, leaving all their stock behind. Moving on, we encountered several other villages all similarly abandoned. Evidently, the bush telegraph had been working well. Finally, we met up with our transport at a prearranged location and moved some distance north into Masai country where I decided to camp, rest and clean up for two or three days.

Coincidentally, this was close to the village of Lemisoi, the tall Masai who was with me when the shifta interrupted our evening meal some years previously. He had been one of the malcontents during the mutiny episode and had never forgotten me forcing him to drink a quantity of milk to try and sober him up. Apparently, to a Masai, this has some special significance. He took me to meet

RHINO

his father who was a local chief and I sat in a dark, smoke-filled hut listening to Lemisoi relate to his father and fellow elders all the adventures and experiences that we had shared since training in England. The old men sat round the edge of the hut grunting their satisfaction, asking the occasional question, sometimes glancing in my direction, and sucking meditatively on long straws which led to a large earthenware pot of warm beer in the centre of the room.

Nothing happens fast in Masai lore and it took many hours to finish the story. Then followed a long and animated discussion after which Lemisoi beckoned me outside and explained that his father and the other elders wanted to give me a bull. I was taken aback because the Masai value their cattle above all else. It was a great honour. After a long pause for thought I asked him what they would say if we killed it and had a big feast with all the soldiers and all his people, explaining in mitigation that if I took it home to my small garden it would probably die of hunger. His face fell. That would be sacrilege. However, he agreed reluctantly to put it to the old men. Predictably, there was a shocked response and some of them even put down their beer straws. The discussion that followed went on for many more hours, obviously relished by all concerned until eventually, to my surprise, they agreed.

That night, we had a memorable party at our camp. We gorged ourselves on the bull and drank nearly a truck load of beer. Then they danced and I played my piano accordion. At midnight we filled the sky with illuminating flares fired from our mortars and Verey pistols, roused the dead with a barrage of thunderflashes and laced the air across the valley with tracers fired from a machine gun on a tripod. Our guests staggered home, well satisfied.

In the morning I emerged somewhat groggily from my tent to find a sombre delegation of Masai elders leaning on their sticks. The leader stepped forward and addressed me:

"*Mzungu* (white man), is it you who was given a bull by Lemisoi's father and killed and ate it?"

"Yes," said I, thinking here come the complaints.

"And are you the *mzungu* who lit up the sky and made all that noise last night?"
"Yes." Definitely complaints.

"And are you the *mzungu* who played the music and handed out the beer?"
"Yes." Defensively, now.

"Well, we are from the neighbouring clan and we have this bull . . ."
I despatched a truck to base for more beer and we repeated the whole performance that night.

The next afternoon I was invited back to Lemisoi's *manyatta* (village) to find the entire population waiting outside. The old man sat me down and made a long speech extolling my virtues. Then an elder stepped forward, asked me to stand, and draped a full-length monkey-skin cloak round my shoulders. The chief handed me a beautiful, symmetrically carved, ebony club, and said, "You are now like a chief. Wherever you go in Masailand, if you take these things, you will be welcome." I must confess that I have never put it to the test.

I n between all these events, back at our base in Gilgil and encouraged by Susie, I was painting as much as possible and selling some too. My subjects were still people based on my sketches and photographs from the north. I was using regular hardboard which I sanded down and treated with ordinary white undercoat. As I became more involved, I realised that there was so much more to learn than the outline lessons I had had nine years before at school. Consequently I purchased a couple of books for beginners which, in some respects, seemed to contradict each other but I did begin to understand a little more about colour.

MASAI WARRIORS

The Masai are a nilo-hamitic people, pastoral and semi-nomadic; their lives revolve around their cattle from whence they acquire their main diet of milk, blood and meat. After the elaborate circumcision ceremony in early puberty, the young men become *moran* (warriors). Some ten years later they will relinquish the rank, shave their heads, join the ranks of the elders, and be entitled to marry.

Traditionally, their warriorhood is a time of colourful adventure when a man must prove himself in battle or some similar act of courage. A common way in the past was to hunt lions. Those who displayed the greatest bravery could wear a lion's mane headdress. Other participants qualified for one of ostrich feathers as shown in this painting. Great attention is paid to coiffure and ornaments and the *Leleshwa* leaves under the arm act as a deodorant.

A friend suggested I should have an exhibition, so arrangements were made with a Nairobi gallery for a date in 1969, which gave me two years to prepare. Then I really started to work and by the deadline I had produced about fifteen paintings, mainly of people but including some landscapes and animals. The show was a near sell-out and for the first time I paused to consider painting as a future career. My time with the parachute company was nearly over – I had been told that I would attend the Army Staff College in England for a year in 1970 – and I had been the only white member of the entire Kenya Army for three or four years. I planned to make a decision after the staff college course which, in any event, would indicate my prospects as a future senior staff officer.

The Nairobi exhibition resulted in a few chance meetings which had a considerable effect on my future although, at the time, I was not aware of it. Perhaps the most significant advice came from the manager of the Wildlife Society gallery who told me I should paint animals, not people. Kenya is a tourist trap and they all want paintings of wildlife. I may give the impression of having a thoroughly mercenary attitude towards my art, but such advice in those days, and indeed now, really struck a chord. My army salary was pitiful, my future was limited and already we had a small daughter, so future school fees were a concern.

Another chance meeting was with a professional photographer, who explained to me the basic principle of thirds in composing a picture. All my paintings had the main subject placed plumb dead centre with the horizon, if there was one, exactly half way. With a few quick sketches he showed me what he meant and I could see the difference immediately. I bought another book, this time on composition, but became confused over "focal points" and "allowing the viewer's eye to lead to its logical conclusion"; so I stuck to the simple "thirds" theory from then on. In the simplest terms, I was led to understand that in a picture of horizontal configuration the main subject should be situated either a third of the way in from the left or from the right. Similarly, the most significant horizontal line (the horizon itself being the most obvious) should be either a third of the way down from the top or a third of the way up from the bottom. My eighteen-year-old son, who is currently studying A-level art, tells me that many of today's experts consider this theory to be rubbish but I still consider it valid and try to follow it as a basic principle both in photography and painting.

I had an interesting discussion about colour with the person who arranged my show. She told me never to use black because it "leaves a hole in the canvas". Out went that tube and I started to use blue and brown instead. She showed me some water colours by a local artist who was colour-blind and could only use browns, reds, ochres and yellows. I was very impressed by this; the simplicity of his colours seemed to add such emphasis to the painting. Perhaps without a conscious decision, I limited my own palette from then on to six basic colours. There was another reason for this: the choice of colours in Nairobi's shops was correspondingly limited.

During our year in England at the Staff College I had little chance to paint. It became evident at a very early stage that I would never be a general. Floundering about in geopolitics, and bewildered at the concept of nuclear warfare in Western Europe, I decided after only a few weeks that I would resign at the earliest opportunity and try painting for a living.

Once during the course we were invited to an "artists' party" where every guest had to bring his own work of art. Of course, most people's efforts were hilariously frivolous but I took it seriously and painted a quick portrait of a small boy which I sold handsomely to a fellow guest. Word got around that I

PLAINS PREDATOR

Mara is supposed to mean spotted in the Masai vernacular. Most of the tribesmen I ask shrug and say, "*Labda*" (maybe) but a few have told me that it refers to the small trees which dot the rolling countryside. This view faces south with the Mara River on the right winding towards the Tanzania border some fifteen miles away.

It is a good area for cheetah although their numbers seem to have decreased as the density of tourist vehicles increases. Interestingly, these beautiful, nervous cats seem to have adapted their routine to avoid the early morning and late evening tourist "rush hours". Customarily, they would hunt at these times, but such activity invariably attracts an instant convoy of noisy, rubber-necking camera-clickers. So now, when the rabble have returned to their lodges in the heat of the day, the cheetahs will hunt in comparative peace.

THE SOLITARY HUNTER

Leopards are among the most adaptable animals in Africa. They are found at sea level in the humid coastal strip, in dry, arid, semi-desert country, and in the highland forests well over 10,000 feet in altitude. The frozen remains of one was discovered preserved in a glacier on Mt Kilimanjaro. A friend was sitting on the verandah of Samburu Lodge having a late night drink after the hordes of tourists had retired to bed, when a leopard calmly walked through the tables and chairs picking up scraps of food from the floor. In my house in suburban Nairobi I sometimes found characteristic pugmarks round my garbage cans. I would equate them to the racoons in America and the fox in Europe in this respect.

When the obscene height of fashion was to wear a leopard-skin coat, it was feared that these beautiful cats were in danger of grave depletion. Numerous research programmes were initiated to ascertain the true situation and I believe the investigators were pleasantly surprised by their results, which generally proved that many more existed than was previously thought.

This leopard is shown in the Ngurman Mountains, a jumbled mass of densely forested peaks and ridges rising to more than 9,000 feet on the western edge of the Rift Valley close to the Kenya/Tanzania border.

could paint and towards the end of the year I was asked to render a portrait of Prince Charles in his uniform as Commander-in-Chief of the Royal Regiment of Wales, for presentation to the college by that year's class of students. Efforts to obtain live sittings were unsuccessful so I travelled to London and acquired a number of photographs from the Associated Press office. I had to admit at the time, and certainly do so in retrospect, that it was not my best work, but everyone was most polite and grateful.

A few months later the Prince visited Army Headquarters in Nairobi, where I was privileged to meet him. Obviously well briefed, he commiserated with me on my task of having to paint his portrait and apologised for not being available to sit. Some time later I understand that he saw the painting in the college and, quite rightly, ordered it to be consigned to the basement.

The only other art work I undertook during that year was a portrait of the Duke of Wellington copied from a famous painting by Sir Thomas Lawrence. This was a fascinating exercise, as I analysed the colours and wondered at my own ignorance.

In Nairobi at the end of 1970 I was appointed to the staff at Army Headquarters. While I was still pondering over the appropriate moment to approach the army commander about my resignation, he called me to his office and announced that I was to be promoted to Lieutenant-Colonel. This would have involved personal presentation of the rank by the President himself, and since I felt an announcement of my resignation shortly thereafter would have been an expression of extreme ingratitude, I told the commander there and then of my intentions. Expressing surprise and disappointment, he said he would discuss the matter with the President.

My request to resign was refused. I was asked to stay on another year and given the position, salary and perks of a Lieutenant-Colonel but, for diplomatic reasons, not the actual rank itself. Secretly I was quite relieved, since the prospect of making my way in the world as a painter was a daunting challenge.

When that year (1971) had gone by I reminded the commander that I should now be released, but he seemed to have completely forgotten. Again he ordered me to serve another year, at the end of which the same thing happened. At last, early in 1974, my persistence was rewarded and I was allowed to go.

In fact the long wait was a blessing because it enabled me to prove to myself once and for all that I could earn a living from painting. Back at the time of my exhibition I had been fortunate to meet the famous wildlife artist, David Shepherd, who was in Kenya on one of his frequent visits. He told me that if ever I was to paint as a profession I would have to treat it as a normal nine-to-five job with no concessions for mood or temperament. With that in mind, during my three-year wait for army release, I painted almost every weekend, concentrating on animals but also taking numerous children's portrait commissions in pencil to keep the coffers topped up.

I spent many long hours in Nairobi National park, studying animals from a new viewpoint, different from that of a hunter, although my previous

IMPALA DOES

CONFRONTATION

This was another of those dramatic colour combinations which demand to be painted. When I found this bull elephant on his own in the middle of a reddish golden plain of red oat grass, he finally lost patience with my persistent presence, choosing the moment when I was half way out of the roof hatch with the engine switched off, to suddenly throw out his ears and blast his way towards the car.

Sketch book, pencil and camera went flying as, instinctively, I performed half a dozen escape actions in the space of a split second, wondering afterwards, when time was less pressing, how on earth I had managed.

The herd behind was artist's licence; his attitude suggested that he should be defending something.

SERENGETI MONARCH

Five million years ago, unimaginable eruptions from Ngorongoro and neighbouring volcanoes produced untold millions of tons of ash which blew westwards, covering mountains and valleys and creating what is now the Serengeti Plains. Over the centuries, wind and rain have eroded the plains, exposing castle-like piles of more ancient rocks which stand like islands in a sea of grass. These are called kopjes (Afrikaans for "little head") and are probably the peaks of long-smothered mountains.

The kopjes have mixed blessings for many animals. Rainwater collects in the rocks, encourages the growth of trees and bushes, and gives sustenance to many species. However, the rocks and trees provide shade, cover and lookout points for predators, particularly lions.

There was an uncanny follow-up to this painting. Long after it was done, I was complimented on the clever way in which I had created a close facsimile of the lion in the large rock to its left rear. I looked at it again and was astonished at what I saw. Certainly, it was quite unintended.

experiences did help a great deal, enabling me to find the animals more easily in the first place, and then to understand their actions and behaviour. Although I had acquired some literature on anatomy, nothing could have taught me more than the physical act of dissecting a dead animal that I had shot.

My work started to sell through a gallery in Nairobi which sent a few paintings to America where they sold for good prices. A number of close friends were professional hunters who, sometimes at the end of a safari, would bring their clients to our house to see what I had and often to order resurrections of the animals they had just bagged. I like to think that their motives stemmed from remorse. By the time I left the army my painting income exceeded my salary. All the same, I was still nervous about taking that step, but the final day arrived and I was free. Scared to death, but free.

As I walked out of the main entrance to Army Headquarters having said goodbye to my many friends, I was approached in the car park by an acquaintance whose company had provided us with military equipment over the years. Over lunch he offered me a job selling his wares throughout Eastern Africa, saying that my knowledge and contacts would be invaluable. When I protested that my intention was to paint he argued that this job would not be a full-time occupation and the short periods when I was required could be very lucrative. Still nervous about earning a living from my art I was persuaded and almost immediately left for Britain to visit defence establishments whose franchises he held.

During the next six months it became quickly apparent that I was the world's worst salesman. The company would call asking me to drop everything and fly immediately to another country where, rumour had it, they were looking for a new battle tank or field radio. Usually, I would decline saying that I was deeply committed to a particular painting but could manage in a week's time. In their world this was unacceptable.

On one of the few occasions that I did travel, it was to Dar-es-Salaam where the Tanzanian People's Defence Force was in the market for fast patrol boats for their navy. In the hotel with me were a number of shady individuals invariably hidden behind large dark glasses, evidently in the same line of business representing other countries. Each evening the Tanzanian officials concerned would make an entrance whereupon there would be an undignified scramble to corner their attention. With my fluent Swahili I got on well at a social level but could do little to satisfy the subtle hints that if a contract were to be signed something extra might be needed. After several nights trying vainly to keep up with my hard-drinking potential customers, my tolerance finally snapped when one of them followed me to the gents' toilet and simply urinated against the wall. I took a long, hard look at the whole grubby scenario, packed my bags and left. So ended my brief and undistinguished career as an arms salesman.

Meanwhile, back in Kenya, I had invested my army gratuity in a small house in Karen, ten miles from the city centre. One of the three bedrooms became my studio and we began to learn the problems created by husband and wife sharing the same house twenty-four hours a day. They were not too serious, but we did tend to hamper each other's normal activities. After a few months a friendly neighbour offered me the use of his guest cottage, which was a much more satisfactory arrangement.

The sudden absence of a monthly pay cheque left a sinking feeling in the stomach for a while, but soon income was arriving from paintings and the phrase: "Paint another picture" became commonplace when any expense above the norm was required.

The most rewarding result of my new lifestyle was to be able to work continuously on a painting from start to finish without having to go to the office. On the other hand, despite my diligence over the previous three years, I soon learned that it required a new kind of discipline to plod on painting day after day. Inspiration for each painting generally followed a similar pattern; total enthusiasm for the first few days when the ideas began to formulate on the canvas, followed by a gradual down-swing as I trudged through the nuts and bolts of the picture, and lastly a renewed burst of eagerness as the finishing touches were made.

A method of painting began to evolve which confounded some of my more knowledgeable friends. Instead of covering the whole canvas initially with a rough wash to give an overall impression at the start, I would begin at the top, painting piece by piece to its ultimate conclusion. For example, I might have a completed background to a point half-way down the canvas, below which there would be no paint at all. Furthermore, there could be blank, white silhouettes within the painted portion where animals would be filled in at a later stage. I stuck with this method for many years until I admitted that there were disadvantages; sometimes the animals looked totally out of place when finally I filled them in. However, on the whole, it seemed to work and at the time, I knew no other way. Possibly, one reason that it did work was that my first drawing on the canvas was always done in meticulous detail.

One of the criticisms which had stuck in my mind from the first exhibition was that the coats of the few animals I had painted were flat and lacked texture. I set about trying to rectify this and, after much trial and error, developed a system which seemed to bring more favourable comment than all other aspects of my style. The answer was to lay the paint on thick and then, using a fine brush squeezed to a dry knife-edge between two fingers, stroke grooves into the paint conforming to the direction of the actual coat hair. This direction was particularly important, for instance, when painting a leopard's coat; each spot had to show which way the coat lay, the yellow overlapping the black on one side and vice versa on the other. I found that if I thinned the paint with a turps/linseed mix the distinction between colours became too blurred and generally the effect seemed to lose brilliance. For that reason I seldom, if ever, used a thinner.

All this sounds most laborious, and it was, but I think that a free and bold style where the paint is laid on almost impressionistically requires great knowledge and confidence, neither of which I had at that time.

During the latter years in the army I had worked closely from time to time with the National Parks, either training within their boundaries as a deterrent to poachers, or arranging basic military training for their own rangers. Consquently, when I retired, I applied to become an honorary game warden, specifically to help on a voluntary basis in Nairobi National Park. Fortunately, I was accepted and two or three evenings a week would patrol the park in an offical warden's vehicle. Primarily, my job was to ensure that visitors behaved in the prescribed manner and obeyed the rules.

It was surprising how stupid some people could be; take, for example, the family who were found placing their small child between their vehicle and a pride of lions in order to take a family snap with a difference. That was complete ignorance, whereas other incidents were not. The big cats were always a favourite attraction and were so used to vehicles that they seldom bothered to move. Several times, drivers of tourist buses were caught throwing stones, waving their arms outside the vehicle, and even driving close enough to nudge the animals so that their clients could obtain the best photographs. On one occasion, a particularly tame female cheetah, who was known for her

WATCHFUL

This female leopard had small cubs hidden in the rocks close by. She takes a precious break from duties to catnap in the sun, free from her ragging, biting, scratching, suckling youngsters and free from the ever-present need to hunt.

The eyes and ears of a cat tell so much about its mood. Her ears in this picture are half back and the eyes half closed expressing awareness of my presence, mild disapproval but not alarm. If I make a small noise, the ears will move further back and the eyes may close in a slow blink as if to say, "Why don't you go away?" A sudden loud noise will cock the ears right forward and open the eyes wide; alert and ready for action. Were I to appear to threaten, the eyes would widen further and the ears would flatten on her head. The greater the danger or threat the wider the eyes and the flatter the ears.

MANYARA AFTERNOON

Lionesses are the stabilizing factor within a pride. They always seem to be the ones who are first to move off and hunt. The lion, himself, will come and go, especially when a female from a neighbouring pride is in season, but the lionesses stay put, are probably all related, and form firm companionships.

The two friends, who look so comfortable in this painting, turned their performance into comedy when they tried to descend. Lions are not natural climbers; although they can go up with comparative ease, coming down presents problems. The animal on the right decided it wanted to climb down but its friend was blocking the way and refused to move despite much nudging and fidgetting. Finally, in frustration, it chose to jump across its reluctant partner, slipped and lost its footing and ended up in an undignified heap on the ground. The left hand lioness woke with such a start from the bouncing and scrabbling behind her, that she too fell off the branch.

readiness to jump on top of cars, had her leg broken by a driver trying to nudge her into action. She was darted, the leg was set and after long months of confinement, she was released. She walked with a limp but later produced six cubs, all of which she raised to maturity, a remarkable feat even for an animal which is 100% fit.

Every time I patrolled I carried a folder containing identification details of all the known cheetahs and lions in the park, each one with a number or name. The lions were identified from the number and positioning of the top row of whisker spots which are never the same in any two animals. Hence, I had a series of lion head profiles for identification purposes. Cheetahs were easier; in their case, it was the ring pattern on their tails. In this way the authorities could plot the daily movement of all these animals, which helped when directing visitors and was also a valuable scientific exercise. If I found any lions or cheetahs I had to stay with them until the park closed. Of course, it was an ideal situation for sketching and studying the big cats, my favourite subjects.

In the mid-seventies there was a severe drought and the wildebeest and zebra which, in those days, migrated into the park from the south for their dry weather grazing, arrived in an emaciated condition. One man's famine is another's feast and the lions lived the life of Riley. They did not need to hunt; carcasses and dying animals were everywhere for the taking. With so much food available the lions' breeding activity seemed to intensify. Months later when the crisis for the plains game was over and food for predators was once again difficult to catch, more than the average number of lion cubs seemed to be born. Unfortunately, there was not enough food to go round and many were abandoned and died. Such is nature.

I was on patrol one evening when I spotted a small animal moving through long grass. Driving closer I was puzzled by its shape and the way it moved. Finally, I realised that it was a lion cub. For the next hour I scoured the surrounding area for signs of its mother but to no avail. When I had relocated the cub, I stopped the car, crept out and stalked towards it but it heard me and tottered away as fast as it could. I gave chase and flung my jacket over it, smothering its spitting, snarling fury.

It turned out to be a female, starving and in very poor condition. I carried her back to park headquarters and was given permission to take her home, at the same time obtaining details of the correct ingredients for feeding. My children were overjoyed and the little animal soon accepted our ministrations and became very tame. That was until feeding time, when she would change dramatically from a playful ball of fluff to a fierce, clawing, growling bundle of rage instinctively warning and fighting off imaginary siblings. It was necessary to wear heavy clothes and gloves if you were the one with the bottle, otherwise your hands would be torn to shreds. As she grew older we had to hand her back to the park orphanage where she would be in professional care. At first they placed her in a special walled-off enclosure within the building which was a ration store for the other orphans. One night, remarkably, she scaled the sheer four-foot-high walls and gleefully slaughtered an entire box of day-old chicks destined for one of the smaller cats. She was found in the morning happy and replete amidst her carnage. She grew fast and it was decided to take her to Kora where George Adam-

YOUNG MALE LIONS

son was conducting his lion rehabilitation programme. She reached maturity in George's care and was duly released, only to be found some months later with a broken leg. They darted her and placed her aboard a light aircraft bound for Nairobi. The story goes that half-way there, to the consternation of the pilot and accompanying veterinarian, the drug started to wear off and only the administration of a booster dose averted an interesting situation.

Her leg mended and she returned to Kora for a second release. Sadly, she has never been seen again but we always hope she survived.

A month or so after my release from the army, I was visited by my good friend, Robert Glen, who, even then, was a highly acknowledged sculptor of African wildlife. He seemed to think that my work was worthy of exhibition at a Texas-based conservation conference which he had attended in the past. The next show of Game Conservation International was a year hence, so I sent off some photographs and was delighted when they invited me to attend. In the short time available I worked day and night to produce ten pieces which I rolled, stuck in a tube and carried with me to San Antonio, assisted on my way by a small loan from the bank and the generous help of the hunter and naturalist, Tony Seth-Smith. Perhaps this was an even more comprehensive acid test as to whether or not I would make it as a painter. The conference coincided with the end of my year's self-imposed trial period so my nervousness increased as the event approached.

I learned a good lesson here on framing. Being on a tight budget I went to the cheapest frame shop I could find but soon realized that I would be paying over the odds because none of my canvasses were a standard size. Instead of picking frames off the shelf, each one had to be custom made. That was lesson one. Lesson two took much longer to learn and even now I cringe from having to select a frame for a painting. The ones I chose for that San Antonio show were appalling, but at the time I was not to know. I thought they were wonderful.

I reported to the conference centre the day before the event was to start and was shown to my three-walled booth inside an enormous hall. Situated round the periphery of the hall were many similar booths with artists already hanging their masterpieces and hundreds of people milling around preparing for the opening. I wandered around in a daze, gaping at the quality of the art and the famous names who were in attendance. Luckily, Rob Glen was there to reassure me and introduce his many friends.

Finally I took a deep breath, unpacked the paintings and started hanging them on the wall. Soon I was aware of a small audience but, with ears burning, carried on with my task. Somehow, this was much worse than the exhibition I had held in Nairobi six years before. On that occasion I had dumped the pictures at the gallery and only appeared briefly on the opening night, suitably fortified. All the framing and hanging had been done by the gallery staff. This was brutally different. One of the most difficult aspects of my new vocation was pricing my work. Advice from well-meaning friends varied wildly and I had no yardstick as far as the American market was concerned. Even today I hate quoting and almost always regret my initial impulsive modesty.

A voice behind me asked the price of the elephant I was putting up. When I told him, he said: "I'll buy it." This was wonderful but somewhat unexpected. Surely the show opened tomorrow? It was then explained that sales were permitted on this day too. I was led to the sales desk and, after completing the necessary documentation, carried on with my task only to be interrupted again, and again, and again. By the time I had them all up, most had sold stickers attached and I had made enough to pay back my loans, cover the cost of framing and my air fare. Overwhelmed is an understatement of the way I felt.

YOUNG ROYAL

Two or three years old, this young male equates in age to a human teenager and, in many respects, behaves the same way. His mane is just starting to grow, he preens and struts, rags and bullies, is overcome by curiosity and frequently gets into trouble by completely misjudging the mood of his elders and betters. Before long, he will be none-too-politely invited to leave the pride, probably in the company of his siblings if he has any. Then he will discover how tough life can be in the big wide world.

ARROGANCE

In certain positions, a cheetah's body is, anatomically, almost grotesque. Its huge chest sometimes juts out so far that I am tempted to think it is deformed. I always think of cheetahs as very serious animals. Maybe it is the facial markings but I cannot imagine a cheetah laughing. A lion could grin and a leopard could leer or sneer but a cheetah would only frown. I enjoy relating animals to human equivalents and would compare the cheetah, perhaps to a dedicated professional athelete whereas a lion would be an amateur rugby player.

I was an emotional wreck. That night was a celebration and I telephoned Susie in Nairobi to say I would not be applying for a job in the safari business.

By the end of the following day I had sold everything and taken enough commissions to keep me busy for a long time. Apart from the auction, I could relax, meet the other artists and study their work. I was pleasantly surprised at their friendliness and helpfulness; one might expect an atmosphere of cautious competition but in every event of this nature that I have attended, the opposite is the case.

I mentioned the auction. At all such gatherings, exhibiting artists are required to donate one piece for an auction, which usually takes place after some kind of gala function where everyone is plied with good food and liquor, no doubt to loosen their purse strings. Perhaps many of them do not realise the agonies suffered by the artists as their individual donations are put under the hammer. In my own mind I know what my painting is worth but seldom does the bidding reach that figure. Luckily mine have always exceeded the reserve price but imagine those unfortunate artists whose work is withdrawn for failing to reach that reserve. After all their hard work and high hopes, it is a cruel, public condemnation; if it were me, I would want to crawl away and hide.

I returned to Kenya, full of enthusiasm and renewed confidence, to continue painting commission work and try to catch up on the growing list of children's portraits. Orders for these were now coming from far and wide including Nairobi's very large diplomatic community, many of whom did not seem to understand that a portrait took time. I was becoming irritated by impatient and sometimes critical parents who demanded that I remove freckles and straighten or fill in crooked or missing teeth. I found it increasingly difficult to keep up with both those and the oil paintings of wildlife and so resolved to phase out the portraits slowly, by accepting fewer commissions.

Towards the end of that eventful year I was asked to paint a large cheetah picture by Geoffrey Kent and Jorie Butler (now his wife). Geoff and I had been at school and Sandhurst together and he now owned the rapidly expanding tour company, Abercrombie and Kent. When the painting was completed, I sent it to the US where, in conjunction with the Chicago Zoological Society, they arranged to have it printed. Later, I flew over to sign the prints which were then sold to raise funds for the Brookfield Zoo, specifically for their new scheme to move animals from the traditional barred cages into more open enclosures where they would be confined by moats and overhangs. They were working on the cheetah exhibit when I was there and I shall never forget seeing a group of handlers and a cheetah in a long corridor where they were trying to ascertain how far it could jump. They needed this information to decide the width of the moat. I could not understand how they intended to make it jump and it seemed an extraordinary way to make such a decision. I offered my humble advice, namely that the width of the moat should depend on the length of the cheetah's run-up. I would love to know their final conclusion.

With the income from San Antonio I bought an old Toyota Land Cruiser specially adapted for safari work, in which, from time to time, I would head for the hills either alone or with the family. Family safaris were great fun although I fear my little daughter developed a slight elephant phobia after we had been charged so many times. If I really wanted to study and sketch the animals I had to be alone; nothing can compare with the feeling of being responsible to nobody and being able to sit, watch and digest everything that is going on. To dwell in one place for hour after hour, hoping to blend with the background, is my idea of peace and happiness. So much stops happening when a large vehicle arrives at any location but if you sit patiently and wait, allowing the inhabitants of that place to forget your initial noise and disturbance, then they relax and carry on with their lives. It is amazing how much of interest can be seen by exercising a little patience.

A favourite camp was in broken country east of the Mara River on a small stream named Olare Orok, well away from the nearest road. I put up my small tent, collected some firewood, cooked my evening meal and settled down for the night. Next morning I was awake before dawn to stoke the fire and boil some water for an early cup of tea. Squatting by the fire in the half light, warming my hands against the night's chill, I had the strange feeling of being watched. Slowly I looked around and from the corner of my eye caught sight of a large male lion sitting on his haunches not twenty years away. He was as overcome with curiosity as I was with alarm. With the hairs rising on the back of my neck, I measured the distance to the car and then to the tent deciding that if he was determined he would get me before I reached either. I took the alternative which was to inch my way round the fire and put my hands in readiness on a branch whose end was burning fiercely. With the fire between us I felt a bit safer, which was ridiculous because if he had wanted, he could have just walked over and grabbed me. But his intentions were not aggressive and after staring at me for a few more minutes he turned and sauntered away, twitching his tail disdainfully.

This was unusual behaviour because lions, particularly in that area where there are Masai, will run away if they see a man on foot. I wondered if he had some intuition that my intentions were peaceable. Small incidents like this leave me in a state of dazed wonderment wishing that every exquisite moment could somehow have been recorded for my perpetual self-indulgence.

After breakfast I tried to cross the small stream behind my camp because throughout the night there had been much roaring and snarling from that direction. I worked out a route for the vehicle, which was easy up to the far bank but then required a steep climb and a sharp left turn to skirt a deep pool and avoid some trees. I drove up the bank, swung the wheel to the left but then realised to my consternation that the rear was sliding back towards the pool. I stopped and gingerly climbed out to assess the situation. If the vehicle continued to slide it would topple over the four-foot high bank and probably finish upside-down in the three-foot deep pool. I climbed in and gently tried to move forward. The back slid another six inches towards the pool. There was no way backwards or forwards without bringing catastrophe. The only alternative was to dig the bank so that the vehicle was on an even keel. Seven hours later I had shifted tons of earth, carried scores of rocks for added traction, and felt completely exhausted. I had one chance to get out and it was with huge relief that I managed. That was a wasted day but the dawn incident with the lion still brought a warm feeling.

The next morning there was ample compensation for the previous day's frustration. I was woken before dawn by the murmuring sound of many voices and the movement of a host of animals. Opening my tent I looked out to see daylight just creeping into the valley and at the limit of my vision a great horde of wildebeest moving in my direction. As the sun came up they invaded my camp in their thousands, paying me scant attention, intent only on moving ever onwards to seek new grazing.

The wildebeest migration is a spectacle that never ceases to instil in me a sense of awe and wonder. They are such strange animals whose lives seem to be one long melodrama, with no-one ever quiet and satisfied. If there is a bull he wants more cows in his harem. At the same time he frantically chases away

SIMBA

A magnificent lion specimen is lying comatose in the morning sun sleeping off a hard night of hunting, roaring, gallivanting and general hell-raising. One of those stinking, noisy, mechanical monsters draws up and he barely opens one eye in acknowledgement, knowing that they are generally harmless. Suddenly, however, he hears the sound of a hyena from the direction of the vehicle and raises his head to bring both eyes and ears into action. The noise persists. Maybe the hyena has found something worth stealing so he rises to his feet, fully alert, peering through the vehicle and ignoring the oohs, aahs and frenzied sounds of multiple motor-drives. The occupants of the vehicle gaze in wonder as the king of beasts, realizing he has been conned, flops back resignedly to the ground and everyone starts talking at once. Some even try to emulate the guide's hyena howl. Regally and disdainfully, the lion ignores them.

HYENAS HUNTING

THE MIGRATION

I had a long-standing ambition to somehow capture the magnitude of the wildebeest migration. At last the opportunity arose to face the challenge on a ten-foot-long canvas. Seldom do photographs of this constant phenomenon do it justice. It is almost impossible to show through a camera's lens the sheer numbers of animals involved because, more often than not, the herds are spread over a flat plain.

One area where this problem could be solved was the Mara where successive low ridges could provide ample space and depth to achieve what I wanted. The positioning of a curious pride of lions in the foreground emphasised the relentless urge of the great herds to move ever onwards.

Once I had recovered from the initial daunting sight of such a vast area of empty canvas, my enthusiasm got the better of me. I determined to pack in as many wildebeest as possible, showing not only the long lines of animals stretching to the furthest horizon, but also the constant dramas which face them along the way; how the crossing of a small bush-fringed stream causes congestion through fear of a predator's ambush; how lions on a kill will simply be by-passed at close range because temporarily they are not a threat. Also I was able to include the many other species for which the annual invasion brings either feast or, at best, disruption; hyenas and vultures, giraffes, impalas, topi, gazelles, warthogs and, of course, the many zebras which themselves take part in the trek.

It was a labour of love and for months I was mentally painting wildebeest in my sleep.

any other bull in sight. The cows themselves never seem satisfied with their own bull and cause him endless concern as they try to slip off to someone else's camp. The calves and yearlings are forever getting lost and yelling their heads off, as are their mothers who can't find them. There's never enough to eat so each little group has to keep setting up temporary home in new locations. If there is a river it has to be crossed regardless of the consequences and more often than not, you reach the far bank only to hear a relative calling you back from the one you have just left. If there is a lake it must be crossed even though it would be much safer to walk round. In many ways they behave like contemporary human society.

One of the most moving experiences I ever had was watching the wildebeest hordes crossing the Mara River. Susie and I were on safari with a friend during a period when unseasonally heavy rain has raised the water level and eroded the banks. The day before we had sat in camp whilst thunder rumbled continuously overhead and lightning flashes lit the sky. The torrential rain turned to hail which lay inches deep on the ground, more reminiscent of a winter scene than tropical Africa.

We found the place where the great herds were building up in preparation to cross and slowly worked our way through the riverine bush to a position which we hoped would be their crossing point. There must have been tens of thousands and the noise was a constant roar of bellowing animals and thundering hooves. We hid below an overhanging bank and waited. Gradually, the leading animals moved closer until they were standing in a great wall on the bank above us. As pressure built up from those behind and the press of bodies compacted, the first brave wildebeest finally plunged in. It was like a bursting dam as thousands blindly followed and the cacophony of voices rose in a crescendo.

Disaster waited on the opposite bank. Erosion had created a steep sill and even if this could be negotiated, there were only two narrow hippo trails sufficient in width to take two animals at a time to reach the safety of the top. The water soon filled with a mass of swimming animals and a few lucky ones started to emerge on the other side. This only spurred the remainder to keep on plunging in. A log jam of animals developed in the water as more and more arrived frantically trying to scramble to dry land over the backs of their comrades. Exhausted, some turned back impeding the flow from our side and finding equal difficulties climbing back out. As the struggle progressed hundreds of animals, too exhausted to swim, simply toppled sideways and drowned. Soon the river was clogged with bodies, but still they kept coming. Suddenly, there was an extra loud thunder of hooves above us and the flow of animals stopped. Cautiously we emerged from our hiding place to peer around and discover a pride of lions not far away, standing on the bank and gazing with mild curiosity at the carnage below. Evidently they had fed well because they soon moved on, and we were able to climb into the open feeling physically and mentally drained by the experience. We had to keep telling ourselves that this is nature's way of controlling population.

In total contrast to the grassy plains and well-wooded watercourses of the Mara is the arid, semi-desert country astride the Tiva River to the north of Tsavo East National Park. This was normally closed to the public but through my association with the warden, David Sheldrick, during my army days, I was given special authority to go there. For most of the year it was hot and dry but teeming with game, especially rhinos and elephants which would dig in the sand of the dry Tiva for water. David had built an elaborate blind on the north slope of the Yatta plateau, a long tongue of old lava which parallelled the

TSAVO RHINO

This rhino painting was based on a sighting in Tsavo National Park East in the days when the warden, David Sheldrik, allowed me to train my paratroopers there. It is typical of Tsavo with its reddish-orange soil and the silvery-white barked commiphera thorn trees. Ironically, both rhinos and commiphera have largely disappeared since then and that part of Tsavo has changed dramatically. The rhinos have all been poached; the trees, which are shallow-rooted and hold quantities of moisture, were destroyed mainly by elephants in times of drought. The countryside was once covered by these trees which monopolised the scant water but once a gap has been created in their ranks, the remainder seem to die off as grass takes over.

THE CROSSING

This was a sequel to "The Migration", another example of my weak will when I had vowed never to paint another wildebeest. However, watching the teeming herds crossing the Mara River some years later, all my former resolve disappeared as my fascination with the hordes of these extraordinary, ugly, idiotic animals once more came to the fore.

Crossing this river is the single most dangerous undertaking in a wildebeest's turbulent year. The wooded banks give cover to predators and crocodiles infest the water, but the greatest hazard comes from too many frenzied animals trying to scramble through too small a gap at the same time. The selection of crossing points is arbitrary and if, as sometimes unfortunately happens, the exit from the water is too steep or narrow, thousands will drown as those in the rear keep surging forward. Nothing can stop the animals in mid-crossing from trampling, jostling and panicking in their efforts to reach the safety of the far bank.

I attempted to create a contrast between the struggling, tension-packed chaos on the left bank and the peaceful greenness of new pastures on the right. The inclusion of a stark, dead tree, vultures, marabou storks, swirling dust and the ominous interest of two hungry lions hopefully emphasised the frantic atmosphere of the thousands still waiting to cross.

Galana River. The blind overlooked a waterhole and it was wonderful to lie in bed watching a great variety of animals come to drink. One morning a pack of wild dogs pulled down a bushbuck at the water's edge before I had even had my breakfast.

Susie and I tried to reach the blind on one occasion but ran into all kinds of problems. We were travelling in a brand new Land Rover and on the way passed through heavy rain storms which rang warning bells because the rivers we crossed led into the Tiva and we had to ford that further downstream. Sure enough, some forty miles on we reached our crossing place to be confronted by a raging torrent. I waded in but was soon up to my waist and in danger of being swept away, so we turned back, planning to spend the night at a ranger post some twenty miles away. We had not gone more than a mile when I noticed the temperature gauge soaring into the red. Investigation revealed that the fan belt had broken and we had no spare. Susie was not wearing tights and her elastic pants proved useless as a temporary measure – so using a Masai sword I cut a fan-belt-sized strip of leather from my bedding roll strap and joined the ends with strands of wire from the towing cable. This lasted five miles before snapping, so I started making another but as I pulled the razor sharp, double-edged sword from its sheath the blade cut right through the side and deep into the palm of my hand. We strapped that up and, many home-made belts later, limped into the ranger post. My hand was a mess so we radioed park headquarters and spoke to David who flew in the next day in his Piper Cub with a new fan belt and sutures for my palm. We never did make it to the blind that time.

Further to the South lies Tsavo West National Park, famed for its Mzima Springs and the location where man-eating lions wreaked havoc with the railway construction workers at the turn of the century. Frequently we stayed with the warden who flew a helicopter which delighted the children and was a marvellous weapon in the anti-poaching war. We were staying with him one weekend with some friends fresh out from England and decided to visit nearby Kilaguni Lodge for a drink. The lodge overlooks a waterhole where I noticed a young bull-elephant standing in a most forlorn manner. Looking through binoculars I could see a wound high on his rump which was probably the cause of his sorry appearance. As I watched, a small herd of dusty, thirsty elephants hurried out of the dry thorn scrub heading purposefully towards the waterhole but as each one passed the sick bull it paused and placed the tip of its trunk gently on the wound as if to console him.

I drove quickly back to the warden's house, told him what I had seen and after he had collected his dart gun, drove back to the lodge. We approached the sick animal as close as possible and then tried to estimate its weight before measuring out the appropriate dose of tranquillising drug. Having fitted the dart to the phial he loaded the rifle, handed it to me and said "Shoot it." The tourists lining the

THE PATRIARCH

TSAVO ELEPHANT

An unusual element of authenticity was added to this painting of a cantankerous elephant in Tsavo National Park. The idea was conceived in Nairobi but when the first layers of paint were still wet, the canvas was thrown into the back of my car and transported through Tsavo itself, gathering on the way a fine coating of real red dust. From there it travelled to the coast where more paint was added, then back to Nairobi for the foreground and, finally, to my studio in England for the finishing touches. A truly international production made all the harder because, prior to this safari, all my paints and brushes were lost in transit, so I had to rely on borrowed materials; somewhat similar to a golf professional having to play in the US Masters with a strange, hastily-hired set of clubs.

DAWN PATROL

A few weeks previously, the hard-packed, dry surface of this great sand river, the Milgis Lugga, was a raging, brown torrent; the consequence of torrential rain in the distant highlands, it flooded incongruously through the semi-desert landscape dwindling away to the east until the last drops disappeared into the dust. A day or two later, the water was gone, leaving intricate runnels and channels reflecting the recent tortuous course of the flood. We followed in its wake with a string of camels marching down the broad highway early each morning before the sun's heat drove us into camp beneath the cool acacias along its banks. Every day at sunrise our headman, dressed traditionally and carrying a spear, and the game scout in faded khakis with rifle slung nonchalantly over one shoulder, would patrol ahead to give us warning of elephants, rhinos, lions or man.

lodge verandah must have been horrified to see someone with a gun deliberately aiming at an elephant in front of their very eyes. I aimed at a flat part of its flank and fired, the dart struck home and the elephant ran off a few yards before slowing down to a halt and, eventually, gradually sinking to the ground.

We drove up quickly and removed an arrow head from the suppurating wound before cleaning it out and packing it with Sulphamezathene. Then came the difficult part. An antidote was injected into a vein in his ear and we waited expectantly for him to wake up. At last he stirred and struggled to regain his feet. An extra nudge from our vehicle finally pushed him up and he tottered away to recover fully. This had been a poacher's arrow but obviously the poison it carried had been old and not sufficiently potent to kill quickly. I had shot my first and only elephant and our English friends had a unique start to their Kenya safari.

With two close friends I planned a return to the north of Kenya with which I had such a close affinity from the days of the shifta campaign. We drove to the remote outpost of Barsaloi and set about hiring a string of camels, for this was to be our mode of transport. After many hours of haggling we acquired three apiece to carry our food, beer, water and bedding for ten days. Each trio of camels had a handler who in turn had his own beast, and finally there was the headman and a ranger/guide. It was an interesting study of values that a camel cost twenty shillings a day but a human handler, only five.

At last we were ready to set off eastwards, following the course of a wide sand river. We had no definite plans other than to return to a certain location to meet our transport ten days hence. It was a magical experience. For the first week we saw no other human being. We marched from 5 a.m. until midday and then took a long siesta, followed by an evening exploration of the immediate surroundings. I was elected cook and disguised my dubious creations, including the porridge, with liberal doses of curry powder. We lapsed into a wonderful life of peace and well-being and refused to contemplate a return to civilisation.

One of the camels fell sick and would not get up despite being roundly cursed and kicked. The handler's equivalent to two aspirin was to work on a good wad of foul-smelling chewing tobacco, and then, with all hands pinning the animal to the ground, spit his evil mouthful up the camel's left nostril. After a great deal of filthy camel language it was not long before the beast of burden got to its feet and marched on, apparently none the worse for wear.

DWARF MONGOOSE

I was truly inspired during this safari and painted, as a consequence, some of my best work. Somehow, the absence of any of the trappings of civilisation such as vehicles, radios and clocks, seemed to make time of no consequence. I could sit and sketch with a completely uncluttered mind. I recall setting up my water colour palette and being mobbed by a swarm of butterflies which appeared as if from nowhere, evidently attracted either by the water or the colours themselves. The sand river was our highway, as much as a hundred yards wide in parts. Its hard-packed surface was moulded into elegant channels and swirls as if

NGURMAN MOUNTAIN GLADE

High in the Ngurman Mountains in southern Kenya there is a large swampy glade on the edge of which I had a favourite camp site. At that altitude, the early mornings were icy cold, but from the warmth and comfort of my sleeping bag I could watch elephant, buffalo and many smaller animals drink and graze before moving back into the shade and security of the high forest during the day. The sun slowly filtered through the valleys lighting up strips of the glade in brilliant contrast to the surrounding gloom and spotlighting any animals, such as this herd of impala, which might be grazing there.

the water which so seldom flowed had been frozen in an instant to sand. Along its flanks grew broad, flat-topped acacia trees contrasting dramatically with the rugged, arid, rock-strewn hills which rose on either side. Early each morning as we headed east with the camels and tribesmen silhouetted against the sunrise, the over-active, romantic side to my nature was indulged to the full.

Two years after my San Antonio showing I returned to the next Game Conservation International conference and happily had equal success. I sold one of the paintings to a co-owner of the King Ranch and was invited there for a few days. They put me on a quarter horse with a western saddle and we rode off with the cowboys to round up cattle in the thick mesquite brush that seems to cover much of southern Texas. I was somewhat disappointed in the cowboys, who were all short Mexicans dressed in T-shirts and baseball caps, but their horsemanship and skill with a rope more than made up for their unimposing looks. I had my first meeting with armadillos which are indigenous, with nilgai (a strange-looking deer imported from Asia which had proliferated) and with a small, seemingly innocuous chilli that looked like a pea and blew the top of my head off.

Later that year I was invited to the World Wilderness Congress where artists from all over the world had been asked to exhibit their work. I was deeply flattered and felt that I was now getting somewhere. Bob Kuhn, the famous American wildlife artist, was there; he and I had already become firm friends at San Antonio and I was excited to hear that he would stop off in Kenya on his way back. Accordingly he, Rob Glen and I set off for the Ngurman Mountains on the western side of the Rift Valley close to the Tanzanian border. This is a wonderful unspoilt range of hills, heavily forested and renowned for its orchids. This trip was a valuable interlude and I gained much from listening round the camp fire to the two masters expounding on the state of art and the world in general.

Game Conservation International held their next conference in San Antonio in 1979 and once more I flew over with a batch of paintings, all of which sold. One of the functions was a visit to a rodeo on a nearby ranch, and during the celebrations I was conned into volunteering to ride a bull. To my horror (overlaid with Dutch courage) the organisers agreed, but thankfully I was only given a steer. All the same, as I sat on its back in the crush trying to persuade it to be gentle, a cowboy was destroying my overtures by tickling its rear with an electric prodder. I wondered at the wisdom of my bravado. The gate opened and I was airborne. We parted company after an embarrassingly short period but long enough for my left arm, which was clutching a rope round the animal's middle, to be stretched an extra two or three inches. One more story to tell my grandchildren. It was only thanks to the timely intervention of a self-styled osteopath that I was able to walk at all next day.

During the conference I was asked by a friend who owned a gallery in

BUFFALO STUDY

Dallas if I was interested in having my paintings printed. Of course I was, so he put me in touch with a firm called the Greenwich Workshop which was based in Connecticut. I met the president of the company in New York on my way home and we hit it off instantly, maybe because he was an ex-Marine. Shortly after that I signed a contract, and my first limited edition prints were released later that year. It was the start of a long and happy association which still exists today. Suddenly my work was exposed to a very much larger market and accordingly enquiries about commissions for original work increased.

During the late seventies I learned a very great deal from my visits to America. Occasionally, I produced a painting which seemed to stop everyone in their tracks and which I knew, as I painted it, was a winner. I tried in vain to analyse the formula for such phenomena but had to conclude that there was no such thing. It had to be a combination of factors, the first of which was impact. To achieve impact I believe simplicity to be an essential ingredient, and contrast another. These sort of imponderables led me nowhere, so I gave up the search for the magic formula, contenting myself with the knowledge that once in a while everything would click.

By picking the brains of more accomplished painters I built up my knowledge of the art. Once I was asked what yellow I used, to which I replied, chrome. The questioner seemed aghast and went on to inquire whether I had ever tried the cadmium range of yellows. To be honest, I had never heard of them and certainly could not remember seeing them on sale in Nairobi. Before my return I purchased several tubes and was amazed at the results when I tried them back home. It was like squeezing liquid sunshine from the tube. More books and more questions revealed a subtle difference between warm and cold colours, and I think my paintings thereafter took on an altogether warmer feeling.

In Nairobi more and more stringent import restrictions were being imposed in order to save the country's precious foreign exchange. Only certain categories of goods, such as agricultural equipment, could be brought in free of duty, and everyone was urged to buy locally produced materials. A customs official informed me that canvas (for tents) and brushes (for whitewashing walls) were Kenya made and therefore could not be imported. I couldn't get round the brush problem – I simply had to stock up when I travelled abroad – but I did import a roll of canvas, designated as material for making tractor gaskets.

I was also becoming concerned that I should diversify and paint more than just wildlife. Being an ardent fisherman, I spent some time trying to work out how I could capture the truly magnificent colours of marlin and sailfish before they faded so quickly after capture. We mulled over all kinds of plans to have me over the side in a cage wearing a scuba tank when a fish was hooked but the complications and expense were too great, and the idea died. I did, however, learn to scuba dive and marvelled at the other world which exists under the sea. Maybe, one day . . .

Sometimes I dabbled in commercial art and designed labels for wine and whisky bottles as well as the outer cover for a wine box. You might have guessed that I had a friend in the wines and spirits business.

Despite these deviations, demand for my wildlife paintings increased, so it seemed the sensible thing to stick with that subject and eventually I even stopped drawing children's portraits.

As my work became better known, there was a corresponding increase in requests for paintings to be donated to raise funds for charity. I am sure this is a difficult problem for all painters. On the one hand, one does not wish to be seen as stingy by refusing to give; on the other, a painting is perhaps a month's salary and how many people would be prepared to give that away? There is no

LAKE PARADISE

Away to the north of Kenya in the middle of a vast, empty semi-desert, rises a massive, forest-covered mountain – Marsabit – famous in recent times as the home of Ahmed, the legendary elephant whose great tusks afforded him life protection under presidential decree.

High in the centre of Marsabit is an ancient caldera whose tree-covered walls slope steeply down to a small lake, aptly named Lake Paradise. For untold centuries this was a haven for elephants, many of them as impressive in size as Ahmed himself.

Since Ahmed's death in the seventies, the price of ivory has soared, poaching has increased and become even more sophisti-cated and Marsabit's great elephants have been cut down to a mere fraction of their original numbers. Civil strife in the surrounding areas has caused a human influx to Marsabit's fertile slopes, and parts of the forest have been destroyed by man and his goats and cattle. The last time I saw Lake Paradise, it was a small muddy puddle trampled by hordes of domestic livestock. Paradise lost?

question of the advantages of publicity but, unfortunately, many charitable organisations dangle that carrot a bit too provocatively, not realizing how much it costs the artist. I still occasionally tot up with some pride the amount I have helped raise for conservation and other causes, but it does not diminish the agony of decision-making when another request comes in. Fortunately, most charitable organisations now realise the artist's dilemma and pledge a percentage back to him.

For four years I was happy to become involved in the world of golf. Each time the Kenya Open was held I donated a painting to help raise funds for Kenya's handicapped children. On these occasions the Variety Club of Great Britain was strongly represented and several times my paintings were auctioned by Henry Cooper, which did my own reputation no harm. As a spin-off I received some commissions, either from celebrities or professional golfers, and even had the privilege to play a short round with Doug Saunders in Houston. His patience was remarkable.

By 1979, I felt a growing but inexplicable frustration. I had developed a small reputation in America but was quite unknown in Europe and felt I needed to be closer to those markets. In Kenya I thought I had almost a captive market with the tourists – maybe I needed to head back to the real world and prove myself. On top of that my eldest child was nearly twelve and I dearly wanted to educate them both at secondary level in England. So, to everyone's astonishment, I announced that we were leaving. Naively, we bought property in southern Spain where I thought the weather and light would be more tolerable. The children would commute to boarding schools in England and I would do the same to Kenya for my material and to the US for my market.

In its simplest form the plan seemed ideal, but we did not reckon with the complications of Spain and ended up in England in late 1979 renting a house on an estate, cheek-by-jowl with hundreds of other identical boxes. For two years we lived in misery, telling ourselves that it would get better, but it never did and in desperation we started looking for a house to buy. At last we found an ideal cottage in a small village with foundations laid for a double garage. We bought the cottage, a dog and a cat, and the garage was built with one half converted into a studio. At last we had a home and for the first time I owned my own studio, and could actually walk out of the front door of the house and go to work.

Surprisingly, during our two years "in the wilderness" I had managed to keep painting. It was satisfying to realise that I could do so even under the most stressing circumstances.

Bearing in mind our new home I decided to see whether I could sell paintings in England. I was introduced to an ex-Kenya farmer who was then the factor for vast estates in Scotland where the gentry go to stalk deer and shoot grouse. One cold week in October when the red deer were rutting, I tramped up and down the Scottish mountains in the wake of the stalkers collecting material for what I hoped would be a new line of paintings. Some weeks later I produced a large rendering of a stag bellowing his challenge with a landscape of snow-covered hills in the background. It received a lukewarm reception at the few London galleries that I approached, so I included it in my next Texas portfolio. Here it achieved little notice and the occasional comment to the effect that it was "a mighty small elk". I brought it back to England and eventually, by pure chance, sold it to an expatriate Scot living in Australia. That episode convinced me that I should stick to the subject I know – Africa.

For years I had wanted to stage a one-man exhibition but there were great problems. It would take the best part of two years to produce sufficient to cover the walls of a gallery, and none of those paintings could be sold in the interim; so what were we to live on? In 1984 I visited a good customer in America,

SERVAL CAT

The beautifully-marked serval cat stands about eighteen inches high and, being mainly nocturnal, is rarely seen in daylight. What it lacks in strength is made up for in stealth. Its huge ears act like radar dishes, picking up the faintest sounds of movement from the hares, rodents and birds on which it preys. In the late evening, one sometimes sees a serval burst from the tall grass in a series of vertical leaps as it tries to spot its quarry.

I have to admit cheating a bit on this painting. The model was semi-tame and wandered freely in and out of a friend's house, curling up and purring before the fire on cold, wet days.

TENSION AT DAWN

From the moment I started sketching out this painting, I knew it was a winner. I could not tear myself away and sure enough, when it was completed, everyone seemed to admire it.

Why? I have asked that question a thousand times, trying to analyse the ingredients for its appeal. Is it the two lionesses, tense and alert, staring fixedly at some potential prey? Perhaps the probability of imminent action draws the viewer's attention. Or is it the colouring? The muted tones of a landscape still in shadow set against the warm brilliance of the lionesses as their faces catch the first sun? Maybe it is a combination of these and the stark simplicity of its composition.

primarily to deliver his latest painting. In the course of conversation I mentioned my ambition and, to my great good fortune, we made an agreement whereby he would advance sufficient funds to allow me time to paint for the show.

It was a new lease of life. The first painting was "Tension at Dawn" – to my mind, one of my best ever creations – which set a high precedent for the remaining nineteen. I must confess that half way through this undertaking the euphoria began to evaporate but I persevered and, by the planned date for the show, had reached my target of twenty major canvasses and forty drawings and sketches.

I felt drained, having concentrated so hard on the task that little thought had been given to the consequences. Suddenly, I panicked at the possibility that few if any would sell at the grand opening. The show took place at the Greenwich Workshop Gallery in Connecticut and thankfully, my fears were unfounded. It was an emotional experience to walk into the gallery and see all my paintings together for the first time. Thereafter, demand for both paintings and prints seemed to increase dramatically. Articles appeared in art magazines, and several paintings were selected for the pictorial edition of Karen Blixen's *Out of Africa*. I looked back over the past twelve years and said to myself: the gamble was worth it.

I consider myself more than fortunate to have found a way of life which is so satisfying and to have had such fun doing so. I love a challenge; so many of my experiences and achievements have happened through a desire to satisfy that urge, some foolhardy, some disastrous, but most paying dividends. My painting accomplishments are due to four main factors; aptitude, an ability to work hard, determination and luck.

Aptitude, or as some may put it, talent, is undoubtedly hereditary. My mother has it; my son too. In order to exploit talent one needs confidence. In a way, it is a chicken-and-egg situation – confidence breeds success but the converse equally applies. In my case, my confidence grew as my work became increasingly popular but no amount of verbal acclaim can match the compliment of someone paying a handsome sum of money for a painting. However, before any exploitation of talent can be achieved circumstances are required to trigger the initial desire to use it. The situation in which I found myself in the army at Garissa was my trigger.

A capacity for hard work is a requisite for any natural aptitude to be developed. I have always enjoyed work and taken a pride in what I can achieve. My years in the military undoubtedly enhanced this ability by instilling discipline. Despite my dislike of routine, I find that I work best to a regular, self-imposed timetable, following David Shepherd's advice which I mentioned earlier. The temptation to take a day off is often there but my conscience always overrules.

I am dubiously blessed with a stubborn determination. I hate to give up on anything. There have been desperate times when I wondered whether I had done the right thing, when paintings have not sold or been inordinately criticised, when the temptation is to back away and do something completely different. But, ultimately, such discouragements act as a spur. This is reflected in my painting regime; I am loath to have more than one painting in progress at any one time, preferring to persevere with each to its final conclusion.

The luck factor was that I should be living in a country where there was a great demand from a transitory population for nostalgic art work. Most visitors to East Africa, whether expatriate workers or tourists, fall in love with the country at first sight. In a small way, I was able to satisfy their demand for a

CHEETAH FAMILY

Young cheetahs have a mantle of silvery-grey fur which gradually disappears as they mature. Their tiny, tear-marked faces are enough to soften the hardest heart. Sadly, the mortality rate is high since they are vulnerable to many predators including the larger eagles. Tourism has done little to safeguard the future of this sensitive and increasingly rare cat. The less they are seen, the more frenzied become the efforts of drivers who do manage to find them. Should a family of small cubs be discovered, their survival becomes doubly precarious. Constant harrassment from vehicles will force the mother to move her young, thus exposing them to other predators, particularly the sharp-eyed raptors. Whilst she moves one of the litter the others will always be in danger. It is now quite rare for more than one cub to be reared to maturity.

memento of Africa. I was also lucky to have spent so many years closely involved with the subjects that I would paint. No amount of formal training could have prepared me better.

Many times, when people see my work, they exclaim: "It looks like a photograph." In most cases I think they mean this as a compliment but it never fails to prick my conscience. I have developed a style which can be described as tight and falls into the somewhat condescending-sounding category of photo-realism. I wish I could have reached this standard without the use of a camera but that would have required endless hours of drawing and sketching and an encyclopaedic knowledge of anatomy. I never had the time, and using photographs is such an easy and convenient option. Seldom do I use just a single photograph; rather, I glean ideas from a large selection. Latterly, I have learned to appreciate the effect of light on a subject, and in many cases I will alter the entire light direction on an animal which I have taken from one of my photographs.

I do not mean to imply that I never draw. Indeed, on safari, I spend as much time as possible with a sketch pad. Rarely will I use only these sketches for the composition of a painting but the value of such an exercise is to force my eye to study every detail of an animal, transferring that concentrated study through my hand to the paper, rather than taking a cursory glance through a camera's viewfinder. The sketch might be very rudimentary but I have mentally noted much that a photograph would have missed.

When asked sometimes if I am an artist, I reply that I am a painter. "Artist" is much too grand and aesthetic a word. I consider myself primarily to be a draughtsman but as time goes by and I labour away at endless intricate detail, increasingly I feel a niggling frustration and the urge to splash out in a much freer and more self-explicit style. It is easy for me to imagine how the famous masters changed their styles so radically from their original realistic routine. Such dangerous thoughts are immediately quashed when reality tells me that I have to make a living in this mad, frenetic world; dreaming must be a thing of the past. On the other hand, I hope that my achievements as described in this book are a mere skimming of the surface. It is a fascinating and rewarding way of life. There is so much more to do.

In 1979 when I left Kenya I had in the back of my mind the thought that it would only be a temporary absence and that maybe, when the children's schooling was completed, we would return. Even so, the knowledge that I

CHEETAH WITH THOMPSON'S
GAZELLE KILL

RESPITE

Lions in love. In keeping with their characteristic arrogance, a mating pair of lions will pay scant attention to onlookers (unless it is another interested male) during their courtship. The couple will separate themselves from the pride and mate frequently but briefly for days. The act itself lasts but seconds and ends with a crescendo of growls, an impressive display of toothy snarls. Then father flops back to the ground looking supremely bored and indifferent whilst mother rolls onto her back ecstatically savouring the last brief encounter. Between their bouts of passion they will lie together in a semi-comatose state of weariness, panting heavily in the heat. It is said that a lion will pant ten times more to the minute by day than by night.

would be leaving the country for such a long period – possibly ten years – was unbearable. Consequently, I racked my brains to find a way of getting back every year, preferably when the European winter was at its height.

Back in the days when I had been throwing myself out of aeroplanes at Abingdon and courting in Dorchester-on-Thames, a little further down the road was a pub owned by the family Binks. Alan was one of several sons who, apart from being an expert on the Spanish guitar, had a passion for Africa, vowing that one day he would get there. Two years later and only a matter of days after Susie and I had moved into our first army house at Gilgil, came a knock on the door and there stood Alan Binks. He had found a job as an assistant on a ranch near Nairobi where the owner was researching the possibility of game farming. I took him hunting a few times and then heard he had moved to a safari outfit in Nairobi where he became a guide. By the time I left Kenya he was recognized as one of the leading safari guides and owned his own business.

Here was my lifeline. We arranged that every winter I would return and help him as an assistant guide on his safaris. Hopefully, my earnings would cover the cost of airfares and I would have the chance to collect additional material for the forthcoming year's paintings.

Fortunately the scheme worked well – in fact, better than expected, because as a bonus his clients would often order a painting. To be honest, I was not a total stranger to the job, having taken commercial safaris out once or twice in the past. However, I soon realised that it was not simply a question of being able to drive across country and find animals, both of which I could do reasonably well. A good guide has to be an ornithologist, naturalist, botanist, mechanic, cook, barman, raconteur, administrator, radio operator, nurse, diplomat and agony aunt to mention just a few. It was not enough, for example, simply to find a lion; one then had to know what it weighed, what it ate and in what quantity, how long it lived, how it made love, what was the gestation period, how many cubs in a litter, and so on.

I envied Binks his ability to store and remember knowledge; my own efforts would stay fleetingly and then disappear, but I think we made a good team since I could always offer our guests the view of a painter in contrast to Alan's scientific contributions. Unintentionally, I speak of this in the past tense; our partnership has blossomed and still thrives. The Swahili word *safari*, literally meaning "journey", has now been imbued with romantic connotations suggesting excitement and adventure. I think we meet up to these expectations by providing a glimpse of how a true safari used to be. This cannot be achieved by simply driving around the more popular and accessible parks sharing the animals with convoys of noisy, sometimes insensitive tourist buses and spending the night in lodges which have all the trappings of any modern, luxury hotel. Hence, we pay over the odds to set up our own camp away from the crowd and, where possible, in areas restricted only to four-wheel drive vehicles. In this way, over the past eight years, we have enjoyed some memorable events . . .

M eru Game Reserve lies to the east of Mount Kenya. We were camped alongside one of the many streams which flow off the mountain. It was early morning and seven of us had just sat down to breakfast in the mess tent. Outside, the camp staff were going about their chores, attending to the tents and preparing the vehicles for an early game drive.

Simultaneously, Alan and I heard the frantic bleating of what sounded like a goat. We looked at each other perplexed since we were many miles from any human habitation. Momentarily, I thought that one of the men had smuggled

WATERBUCK

During my national service a bunch of "squad-dies" were skinny-dipping in a deep river pool during a break from manoeuvres when we suddenly heard the exciting barking of a pack of dogs. Through the bush which fringed the pool burst a large male waterbuck which plunged into the water amongst us and submerged until only his nostrils were showing. The dogs ranged back and forth searching for the scent before we chased them away with a shower of stones and verbal abuse. This is typical waterbuck behaviour. They are proud-looking animals and seem strangely ill-adapted for the heat of Africa with their long shaggy coats which could be more appropriate to a temperate climate.

in his rations on the hoof on the big truck but that was quickly dispelled as the terrified sound came rapidly nearer and shouts of alarm were heard from the men outside. We leapt from our chairs and dashed from the tent in time to see a half-grown waterbuck, about the size of a great dane, staggering towards us dragging something large behind it. The object turned out to be an enormous python which had sunk its teeth into the unfortunate animal's back just above its tail.

It seemed as if the exhausted animal with its grizly burden would run right into the tent, but at the last minute it staggered round the side and collapsed a few yards away in full view of everyone. It was as if the incident had been stage managed. Instantly, the snake encircled it with its huge coils and slowly squeezed it to death, quite oblivious of the large audience which by now had gathered all around. All the women in our group had fled, the men were frantically searching for their cameras and the camp staff arrived in force, armed with the nearest weapon they could lay their hands on.

As soon as the victim stopped struggling, the python appeared to realise it was not alone and, quickly disentangling itself, slithered away to the nearest cover, scattering people as it went. It must have measured close to fifteen feet but even so, it was incredible to think that it would have swallowed that whole waterbuck had we not been there. To my mind this was one of several occasions when an animal whose options have all run out will seek help from its ultimate enemy, man, as a last resort.

Heated discussion amongst our camp staff followed the snake's disappearance with everyone offering his own advice loudly at the same time. Opinions varied as to how to dispose of the body. The less squeamish wanted to eat it; the more superstitious swore that those who did would, in turn, be eaten by the snake as they slept in their beds. Others wanted it dragged far away convinced that the python would return to claim its spoils and would seek retribution on those who had disturbed its meal. In the end we did remove it some distance from camp and repaired to our interrupted breakfast although, I have to say, some of us seemed to have lost our appetites.

I have been chased many times, both on foot and in a vehicle, by angry elephants and I treat these great beasts with a deal of respect. Twenty or thirty years ago one could rarely approach a herd closely. Either they would flee or more often than not, would display aggressively. I am told that ninety-nine percent of the time an elephant's threatening display is all bluff. I am sure that is true, but for me, discretion is always the better part of valour and I prefer to keep to a safe distance. My partner, on the other hand, often seems to have a death wish and will drive to within a few feet, switch off his engine, stick his head through the roof hatch, and calmly take pictures even though the elephant might be shaking its head and waving its trunk in anger. Maybe it is because he has had more experience with the now gentle animals which have matured in constant proximity to tourists.

Perhaps, however, my timidity is on the wane. I am writing this just two weeks after a safari incident which left me with little option but to face up to elephants literally at arm's length. My vehicle had solenoid trouble and, on occasion, failed to start. The remedy was to crawl underneath it and, with a screwdriver, short two parts of the electrical system. I stopped at a respectable distance to watch a small group of elephants, and switched off the engine. The animals slowly and peacefully grazed to within fifteen yards of the car paying us no attention as we quietly took pictures. Then my nose started to tingle and, before realising, I had blasted out a loud and unrestrained sneeze. The effect was dramatic. The elephants were galvanised and, wheeling as one, charged

SAMBURU ELEPHANTS

In Samburu Park this small herd of cows and calves, surprised in the dense thorn scrub near the Uaso Nyiro river, bunch together for protection, the mature animals alertly facing outwards to shield their young.

The recent history of Samburu's elephants is a tragedy. To the east and north, the vast emptiness of the northern frontier stretches to the distant borders of Somalia and Ethiopia where *shifta* bandits, Somali poachers and the ravages of war have decimated the once extensive elephant populations. Traditionally, they migrated freely to and from the reserve depending on the availability of water, but with certain death awaiting them to north and east, the remnants moved west into the highlands, invading farms and ranches. The herds were harrassed and scattered further afield, many falling to poachers and farmers, some managing to reach the sanctuary of the Aberdare National Park and the remnants returning to Samburu.

A small but stable population now exists here, sadly a fraction of its former size but able to subsist on the marginal food available within the reserve.

FATHER CHRISTMAS

I never could find out why this distinctive old bull elephant was called Father Christmas, but for some years he was a well-known, if sometimes unwelcome, resident of the area close to Meru National Park headquarters. Visitors to the park would soon recognise this irascible old patriarch if they stopped to take his photograph, when he would push out his ears and furiously charge their car.

They say an elephant never forgets. I wonder what incident in the past caused this irrational behaviour. I wonder also where he is now, so many years after his antics caused such alarm and excitement.

I painted this before compositon became an important factor in my planning, when the subject was placed in the centre of the canvas. If I had to do it again, I doubt whether I would change it. The old elephant seems just right where he is.

towards the car led by the matriarch with head high and ears outstretched. My hand flew to the ignition but, of course, nothing happened. Not the time to get out and start fiddling with a screw-driver. My two clients and I sat in frozen agonized anticipation as the elephants halted only yards away, stared down at us indignantly, decided we were not a threat, and continued with their feeding.

Mentally, I filed away the interesting fact that elephants are averse to loud sneezes, at the same time struggling to regain my composure in front of my somewhat shaken visitors. Meanwhile, as the elephants showed no inclination to move away, I noticed dozens more moving towards us from the surrounding acacia woodland. All thoughts of starting the car were abandoned as we were soon surrounded by more than fifty elephants.

Inadvertently, we seemed to have chosen a point where several small herds met to exchange views and pass the time of day. There was much congenial milling about all around the car, with newcomers gently placing the tips of their trunks in the mouths of those already there – a common form of elephant greeting.

Then onto the scene came Miss Fancy Pants herself, a young female obviously about to come into season, friskily flaunting herself at all the young bulls. These youngsters respectfully moved aside as several huge, mature males arrived to solemnly investigate the small mountain of dung which the lady in question had indelicately and inconveniently deposited two yards from my window. Each bull in turn examined her thoughtfully at both ends, seemingly came to the same conclusion that she was not sufficiently ready, and casually moved on. The rudely scorned female then manifested her fury by stripping a six foot length of acacia bark from a nearby tree, holding one end in her trunk and rushing about whipping not only her own flanks but those of any other elephant in range. When this antic still failed to gain attention, she petulantly flung her toy away, stood stock still and stared calculatingly at our car. You could almost hear her thinking that if no-one else will have me, maybe this strange object will. Suddenly, she kneeled down on her front knees (elephants have knees front and back!) and shuffled towards us until her tusks were under the front fender. With some alarm I began to wonder if shortly we would need more than just a screwdriver to get us started, but she backed away, shook her head in disgust at our lack of response, and wandered away to join the herd. Collectively, we let out a long breath. I turned the key in the ignition and the engine started.

I love the way elephants seem to play games with people and how apparently they can differentiate between blacks, browns and whites. There was one famous, racist old bull in Amboseli who passionately hated Asians and would charge furiously at any vehicle in which they were sitting. One wonders what it was in the past that provoked his phobia and how he could tell when Asians were present. Others seem to take a mischievous delight in frightening people knowing that a good, close-range trumpet can unsettle the coolest head . . .

I was driving through Lake Manyara park in Tanzania along a narrow forest track with four excited and hopelessly unruly children in the back. It was our first day out and I had drawn the short straw, driving the nursery car. Rounding a bend we found an elephant blocking the road. Despite my whispered orders to keep quiet, the four hooligans clambered through the roof hatch exclaiming excitedly about their first elephant. He, in turn, stood his ground and took stock of the situation. I inched forward a few feet and he slowly turned to walk sedately up the middle of the road. I followed at a discreet distance as he turned his head slightly to glance back at us from time to time. When he stopped, I stopped, for all the world like a game of Grandmother's Footsteps. This charade went on for several hundred yards and it was evident that the elephant was thoroughly enjoying my frustration at not being able to pass. Finally, he climbed the low bank on the right of the road and wandered off a few yards, casually picking at a nearby bush. I eased slowly forward but just as I reached the critical point where I could accelerate past, he dashed back into the road and resumed his stately progress. Twice more he taunted me this way, and the noise from behind increased as my charges relished the game. Finally, my patience ran out and when he next left the road I flattened my foot to the floor and shot past. He was furious at being caught out and flung himself towards us as we drew level, ears flapping, trunk out, emitting an earsplitting blast at point blank range. The kids fell into the back seat in a tangle of arms and legs suddenly silenced by the proximity of the elephant and overwhelmed by his trumpeting. After that they seemed to realise that we were not in a zoo and I quietly thanked the elephant for helping me regain control.

I n Ngorongoro crater one can find perhaps the last of the great tuskers. The very nature of this vast amphitheatre, surrounded on all sides by high escarpments where the guardians of its treasures can keep a constant lookout, is a deterrent to would-be poachers. Here is a handful of the last survivors of the giants that used to roam throughout the continent. I sit and watch them with awe and sadness, knowing each time that it might be the last chance ever to see such ancient magnificence.

Alan and I parked our respective vehicles strategically in the path of a venerable tusker who was plodding slowly and laboriously across the open plain. A vehicle from another outfit drew up behind us and the occupants of the three sat in respectful silence as the giant moved ever closer; twenty yards away he halted standing motionless for several long seconds as he assessed the situation to his front. Then, very deliberately, he moved forward, not to one side but directly towards the vehicle behind me. Ten yards to go and the driver lost his nerve, started the engine and reversed hurriedly away. As he did so, the aged elephant quickened his stride, threw out his trunk and shook his massive head, dislodging a cloud of white dust. One could imagine him raising the equivalent of an index finger and chalking up one success. This was obviously a fillip to his elephantine morale.

Having reached the recently vacated position of the rear vehicle, he paused and I could see him sizing me up as success number two. Gritting my teeth, I was determined not to chicken out in front of Alan, and waited in suspense for the inevitable to happen. Sure enough, he turned and started towards us with concentrated deliberation. The gap closed to ten yards; still he came and still I sat tight, knowing that my partner was gleefully willing me to crumble. At five yards the elephant realised that we were calling his bluff, so once again shaking his huge head and blowing a half-hearted, frustrated trumpet, he wheeled and sauntered away as if nothing had happened. In the back of my car the occupants, who had long since abandoned the roof, let out a multiple exhalation of breath as I stuffed my hands in my pockets to stop them shaking.

In many parks now one can still see large herds of over a hundred elephants. Perversely, this is not a good sign; instead it indicates stress as these animals, when threatened, will congregate in large numbers for mutual protection. It saddens me these days to see such large herds move rapidly away when approached, a sure sign that someone has been shooting them from a vehicle.

DUSTY ELEPHANTS

As a boy, I would avidly read books on the exploits of the famous "white" hunters whose names have now become legend. I suppose that in our current age of conservation consciousness, they would be castigated as ruthless, commercial destroyers of a precious dwindling heritage but I believe their love of nature and wildlife was paramount and, were they alive today, their efforts would be in the forefront of the fight to preserve.

Many of their stories relate to elephant hunting and the quest to bag the almost mythical giant tuskers. Often, these wise old patriarchs would keep constant company with several younger bulls who seemed to act as courageous guardians of the elder statesmen. Many is the tale of a hunter being charged by these young protectors.

I am not aware whether this alleged trait is recognised by the boffins as proper elephant social behaviour but, in any event, it's a good romantic notion which I have attempted to depict in this painting from Amboseli under the shadow of Mount Kilimanjaro.

YAWN AND STRETCH

How would you like to hang on your wall a painting of an animal with its mouth wide open? This question vexed me for some considerable time before I undertook the subject. Would you not be tempted to yawn every time you passed it? I am still not sure of the answer. If I owned a portrait of someone roaring with laughter, I think I could be driven to cover his mouth after living with it for some years. Despite my misgivings I chose the leopard in this pose primarily for its classic lines which so clearly show the power, agility and impressive fangs of this beautiful cat.

THE OLD WARRIOR

In a marquee erected in the grounds of an elegant country house near Oxford, I stood with easel and palette, cordoned off by ropes for three days from the general public who filed past and watched me paint this old lion. This was part of an arts festival in which I had been invited to "perform". It was a harrowing and unnerving experience and I yearned for the solitude of my studio or the peace of the African bush. A hundred times or more I must have been asked where I kept my model and each time I pointed solemnly to a matchbox on a nearby table.

Not one of the thousands who saw the painting develop asked why the lion had one ear, a fact which I found remarkable. He lost it in one of his many fights, hence the title "The Old Warrior".

Since I was a boy I have always had a love-hate relationship with baboons. I have seen the havoc they can wreak on a field of maize and the brutal way they can tear a dog to pieces should it be foolish enough to take them on. Yet I can sit and watch a troop of baboons for hours fascinated by their complex social behaviour and marvelling at their similarity to humans.

In many of the parks they have become so accustomed to humans that they are not only a nuisance but sometimes positively dangerous. In my warden's vehicle in Nairobi National Park I once took my wife and her mother to a well-known lookout point on top of a high cliff where it was permitted to leave the vehicle and admire the view. The rocks were home to large numbers of hyrax which would rush up fearlessly if one rustled a bag of potato crisps. I stepped to the edge, rustled the bag and was somewhat suprised when a full-grown male baboon bounded up the cliff, leapt over the railings and hurled himself at my outstretched hand. Instinctively, I hid the bag behind my back but then he leapt right at me, forcing me hurriedly to hand it over and beat a hasty retreat. He grabbed the crisps and disappeared. I was left shaking with fury, to be roundly scolded for my stupidity by my women folk. I was guilty of breaking one of the park rules which forbids the feeding of baboons. They become so familiar and daring as to be dangerous and, from time to time, drastic steps must be taken to discourage them. The next day, alone, I returned to the same spot armed with another bag and the jack handle hidden in my other hand behind my back. I rustled the bag and, for once, was dismayed to see all the hyrax run out of their holes to greet me. I never did get revenge.

YOUNG BABOONS

On a fifty-foot-high bank overlooking a river I was quietly sketching. The opposite bank sloped gently down to the water below and was a favourite drinking spot for a variety of animals. As I sat hidden from view a troop of baboons swaggered down to drink so I thought I would have a bit of fun. The warburgia tree under which I was hidden was dropping a hard, green, plum-sized fruit so I hurled one of these across the river and it plumped into the sand beside a large male baboon who had been grubbing about in the dirt. He froze for an instant, stared fixedly at the fruit and then lifted his head to look up into the tree from whence it had come. Uh-oh, no tree! He gazed off at the nearest tree – at least twenty yards away – then back at the fruit, then up again. By this time I was laughing so hard that it was difficult to lob any more fruit. The puzzled animal could not work out how the berries could drop from the sky – he never did discover and eventually walked away in disgust.

One of the frustrations of a guide on photographic safaris, especially in places where there is heavy tourist traffic, is animals which have become so inured to car loads of noisy, camera-snapping people that they exhibit attitudes of supreme boredom, indifference or simply lie down and sleep. The laws are strict: no disturbing the wildlife. Some of the more unscrupulous drivers ignore such strictures and will go to any lengths, sometimes with tragic consequences, to obtain that dramatic shot for their passengers. The most infamous case concerned a leopard which was physically flushed from a thicket by a pack of minibuses, fled across open country to reach safer cover and ran straight into a pride of lions which killed it.

I have listened with amusement to the sounds of hopeful encouragement coming from spectators round a sleeping pride of lions: "Kitty, kitty kitty! – woof, woof! – miaow! – pssst! – grrrr! – smile! – hey! – boo! – Hey buddy, ferchrissake do something!" The drivers will hoot their horns and the passengers will make tempting little kissy noises but the lions will simply keep on sleeping.

One needs a more subtle and thoughtful approach. Lions and hyenas co-exist in an atmosphere of uneasy truce each realising that they rely to some extent on the other. Lions will scavenge hyena kills and vice versa and so each will pay careful attention to the scent or sound of the other's hunting activities. Hyenas have a weird and extensive vocabulary, the most common call being a "whooo-oo" starting on a deep note and ending abruptly on a high, a familiar and somewhat eerie sound of the African night. If I am in good voice, I can produce a passable imitation. I feel a fool doing it in company but it has been known to bring lions to their feet staring curiously at the cars. The camera shutters click like machine guns.

I can also produce a wildebeest's toneless cross between a bleat and a moo. This works well with lions who are accustomed to a seasonal wildebeest bounty when the migration arrives. If it is not the season the lions will sit up and stare in bewilderment into the distance hoping that the good times are back once again.

A leopard lying immobile high in an acacia tree nearly fell off his perch on hearing the alarm call of a vervet monkey. He bounded through the branches until he was standing almost above us and glared fixedly towards what he thought was the source of the noise – not, I feel, that he was after the monkeys but that he feared an intruding leopard had disturbed them. More exciting photographs.

The most fascinating and rewarding example of attracting animals by this method happened when I was walking in the Loita Hills. Ahead of me I saw a group of banded mongooses, busy little animals which forage across the plains frequently standing on their hind legs to see over the long grass. I froze behind

a small bush and started making a high-pitched squeak similar to a small animal or bird in distress. The mongooses all stood up looking for the source of the noise. Then, as one, they moved towards me, stopping every few yards to stand and scout. Eventually, they were standing in a row just a yard

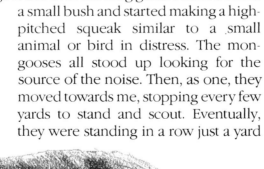

THOMPSON'S GAZELLE

CHUI

The Swahili word for leopard.

I chose this painting as the basis for my only attempt at an original hand-drawn lithograph. This involved close cooperation with a master printer and required me to draw on semi-opaque plastic eight originals of the same subject, each one corresponding to a specific colour. Take, for instance, yellow; the relevant drawing would only show in pencil where yellow was required on the master print and the pressure exerted by my pencil would dictate the intensity of that colour. By complex technical means, the drawing was etched onto a plate which was then used in the press to print yellow onto the paper. Another drawing represented brown, another black, and so on, until all the colours superimposed produced "Chui". A labour of love, and an exercise in the technologically modified version of a centuries-old process.

STALEMATE

An hour after dawn we found these three exhausted animals in a state of near-stalemate. The two lionesses must have bayed the old bull buffalo at sunrise and, taking turns to attack his front and rear simultaneously, reduced him to a weary but still defiant standstill. His flanks were bloodied but he still had strength to ward off the flagging assaults.

Later, I recreated the drama on canvas, hoping to give the impression that it could be anybody's victory.

In reality, the buffalo lost all his options when a great, shaggy-maned lion came loping across the plains to join the battle. He stopped ten yards from the antagonists, assessing the situation for long seconds, and then charged forward, leaping high onto the buffalo's back. He reached round to seize its muzzle with one huge paw and wrenched it up, felling the big bull in a trice. Instantly, he pinned its horns to the ground with his paws and covered the muzzle with his own mouth. As the bull slowly suffocated, the lionesses attacked its nether region in the most unladylike manner.

away mystified by the strange sound until, suddenly, they realised their mistake and fled in panic.

The dry weather had seemed interminable. The grass was yellow and sparse and dust devils raced across the plains. On the horizon, however, the clouds built up and the air was thick and stifling with humidity. I chose this time to drive to the Mara from Nairobi and my arrival coincided with the first torrential downpour of the long-awaited rains. The dusty black cotton soil turned to glutinous, cloying mud through which I found a herd of buffalo being chased by a single lioness. One cow lagged behind and, realising she was in trouble, turned to face her attacker. The buffalo tried vainly to follow the circling lioness which chose a moment when the tired beast was off balance to move in and hit it with one paw on the side of the head knocking it over sideways. It was an extraordinary sight and the sound of the blow rang like a pistol shot. In an instant the lioness grabbed the buffalo by the muzzle, suffocating the unfortunate animal by closing its nose and mouth. The main herd by now had stopped and several large bulls trotted back to help their fallen mate. This, I thought, was going to be high drama. The bulls charged forward, craning their necks to sniff at the tail end of the fallen animal, pawing the ground and snorting as they did so. The lioness still hung on and I was surprised when the buffaloes suddenly ran away. Usually, they will attack a single lion. It could have been that they felt insecure and handicapped with football-sized lumps of mud sticking to their hooves.

Then I realised that there were other lions following. Obviously taking advantage of the soggy ground, they continued the chase of the main herd. In the next ten minutes, three more buffalo were killed, far more than the lions needed. I made a mental note of the deep bellow a buffalo made when it was pulled down and the next day, tried an imitation on another pride. At once, lions were on their feet trying to find out where the buffalo was dying. My clients looked at me in a rather strange way but appreciated the lions' reaction.

Recently, I found a pride which was totally unmoved by any of the vocal noises I could produce. In disgust, as I was moving away, I barked like a dog and immediately the nearest lioness sprang up and backed away, ears laid flat and lips curled in a spitting snarl. It took me a few moments to analyse her reaction; in that area, lions live in proximity to and in fear of the Masai who rely on their dogs to warn them when the big cats approach their cattle or villages.

MANGY OLD LION

Trogon Camp is situated on the narrow neck of a big ox-bow bend of the Mara River. A trogon is a brilliantly-coloured, shy, forest bird and the resident pair were very much in evidence when I spent an idyllic month there, sketching whatever I could find in the surrounding area in the early mornings and late evenings, and painting in my bush studio during the day. Standing at my easel I could look down

TALL SHADOWS

My aim in this painting was to recreate that special atmosphere of lazy peace so often experienced if one takes the time just to sit in one place and patiently watch. After a while one's presence will be accepted and animals and birds will once more resume their daily business. The rich chestnut and white coats of the reticulated giraffes seemed to blend so well with the wonderful light and shade effects produced by sunshine on the bark of yellow acacia trees. By virtue of their height, I have always found it difficult to fit giraffes into a pleasing composition but here, by angling their necks progressively from the upright, stretched posture of the left hand animal to the forty-five degrees of the one on the right, I attempted to break up their normally vertical configuration. The right hand giraffe peers quizzically at a pair of peaceful, ruminating Grant's gazelles which underline the impression of peace and counterbalance the taller subjects on the left.

TAWNY EAGLES

Simon Combes
Jul 87 ©

BUFFAWALLOW

Contrast. It gives such impact to a painting. Here it is evident in both subject and technique. This is the driest time of the year as shown in the drab, bleached background colour and that mood is somehow accentuated by the really wet wetness of the muddy pool where the buffaloes have come to drink. The dark colouring of the animals stands out starkly and emphasises their vulnerability.

I focus my attention on the nose of the foremost bull as he stands poised for action in the mud. One small contrasting splash of white on its black surface makes it glisten and live. Other minute light-coloured droplets below its chin describe how, in alarm, it has just wrenched its muzzle from the water to point it menacingly in the direction of suspected danger.

steep banks at the slow-flowing water on either side. In a short time the resident animals grew accustomed to my presence and went about their daily business without fear. Every afternoon I had an attentive audience of baboons; the youngsters would slowly creep up behind me overcome by curiosity and, if I turned round, would scamper back a few yards. I would often indulge in a game of head bobbing which, in baboon language, means: "Who the hell are you, why are you here and what are you going to do about me?", or words to that effect. The young baboons would bob back at me, puffing themselves up threateningly and uttering falsetto barks of alarm. Usually they would find a small bush to hide behind and violently snatch down twigs and leaves in a display of juvenile indignation.

In the river itself were hippos and the constant, sucking "plop" of big catfish. Several elephants were permanent residents including a cow with a tiny calf. One afternoon there was an ear-splitting scream behind me. My brush smudged across the canvas, I jumped out of my skin and turned to see a lion sprint past, paying me no attention. More lions came running from the sound of much crashing and trumpeting in the bush. By this time I had clambered on to the roof of the car, puny paintbrush held like a sword, palette like a shield. Suddenly, the mother elephant burst into the open, screaming at the lions which must have come too close to her baby. She rushed around the camp furiously charging every bush until she was satisfied that the intruders had been well and truly routed. Then calm returned; I saw no sign of the lions, so descended from my perch to repair the smudge on my painting.

A few days later I looked up from my work to see a new elephant, one I had not seen before, standing quietly only yards from my easel. He had crossed the river to my side on the outer curve of the ox-bow and wanted to pass through the narrow neck where I was working. To do so he would have to pass within five yards of me or go back the long way round. I held my breath as he shifted silently from foot to foot, carefully weighing up the situation. Finally, he moved forward and past me, watching intently as I stood motionless. Such rare incidents of trust between man and wild animals give me a great thrill.

Sometimes one is fortunate to witness a sequence of events which, although commonplace, is rarely seen. One such happening took place in the evening when I was watching a pride of six lions waking from their long day's rest, stretching and yawning prior to a night of hunting. Suddenly they all flattened into the long grass, looking intently past my vehicle. Glancing round I saw a warthog, tail erect like an antenna, trotting purposefully towards us. It was getting late and he was obviously anxious to reach his burrow before night fell. The lions fanned out in a line, snaking through the grass with their bellies flat to the ground, almost invisible from a few yards distance. Twenty yards away the warthog stopped, head held high, sniffing the air aware that danger was imminent. He must have caught a whiff or a glimpse of lion because suddenly he galloped off at a tangent like a bat out of hell. The last lion in the line erupted from the grass and charged a few yards to intercept the hog, pulling him over with one massive forepaw and fastening his jaws on the warthog's throat. The others raced over to grab whatever they could.

The transformation was dramatic, from a lazy, friendly, united team to a snarling, growling, scratching, fighting whirlwind of frenzied individuals each intent on denying the others' access to the kill. Moments later a hyena appeared, trotted close, lowered his half open jaws close to the ground and then, suddenly raising its head, emitted his characteristic "whooo-oo" howl.

As we looked around in the growing dusk other hyenas could be seen running from all directions and within minutes there were twenty or more circling the lions in a highly agitated state. The noise increased as the lions tore at the carcass and each other and the closing hyenas set up a chorus of extraordinary sounds which seemed to bolster their courage. One or two of the braver hyenas would dart in and nip the flank of a lion which in turn would whirl and lash out before hurling itself back into the fray. As the offending hyena fled, the others would surge forward, hoping to exploit the gap in the lions' ranks.

Several hyenas now seemed to unite as, shoulder to shoulder, tails raised and whooping ever louder, they advanced on the lions. Each time the wall got too close a lion would spin round to scatter them but immediately they reformed and advanced again. Finally, the lions wavered and withdrew with much growling, tail-lashing and short charges at the intruders. The remains of the warthog were engulfed by a tide of hyenas, each snatching whatever it could and running off. One had a leg in its mouth and ran around our car howling and looking over its shoulder at four or five others which were in hot pursuit. So intent was it on looking back that it failed to notice one of the lions in its path and was knocked flying by the haymaker swipe of one huge paw.

As the skirmishes died down I looked at my visitors, who were still agog and not quite believing that the whole drama had taken just ten minutes, and all because a silly warthog was late getting home.

I cannot finish this book without mention of gorillas. In 1987 I was fortunate enough to take some clients to the Parc des Volcans in northern Rwanda where Dian Fossey undertook her famous research on the mountain gorillas. My presence there was really superfluous because the local guides are more than competent but I was anxious to go, if a little sceptical because I had heard that the whole experience was somewhat regimented. My fears seemed well founded as we were marshalled and herded into groups, but at last we set off for the high forests where the remnants of these great apes live.

After noisily crashing around in the bamboo and giant nettles for more than an hour with the guides talking and joking I began to wonder if any animal would allow such a rabble to approach. But suddenly the atmosphere changed, the guides stopped jabbering and moved forward quietly, occasionally uttering a short coughing grunt. Then the head man was beckoning us forward and we found ourselves surrounded by a family of big, black, hairy primates. They seemed quite unperturbed by our presence and carried on munching at the vegetation. At times, they were only a yard or so away and I was struck, more than anything else, by their eyes; a reddish amber in colour and seeming to have no pupil.

There was a gentle luminosity about them which defies description and when they looked at me, it was as if I was not there, rather, they were looking right through me. There seemed to be an aura of great wisdom and timelessness about them and, as a human being, I began to feel very stupid, gauche, clumsy and insignificant. I wish we could have stayed for days and can well understand how people who have had long association with these extraordinary, gentle and intelligent beasts become emotionally obsessed.

My American friends returned to the forest the following day. There was a bureaucratic mix-up in the bookings so I volunteered to forgo another trek to the gorillas. Standing in the cold dawn at the foot of the mountains, I asked one of the guides what else there was to do. He pointed high up to the 12,000-foot, mist-shrouded peak of Mount Visoke and said that, for a small consideration, he would take me up there. It was on the slopes of this mountain that Dian Fossey conducted her turbulent and controversial programme so I clinched the deal and spent the next five hours fighting for every breath as we clawed our way

MOUNTAIN GORILLAS

When I visited the mountain gorillas in Ruanda, I was impressed, more than anything else, by their facial expressions and individuality. I determined to try and focus on this when I undertook the painting and so, from the start, more than one gorilla was a prerequisite in order to have a range of expressions.

Having completed the picture, I was asked what the three gorillas were thinking. Well, imagine three people sitting in an elegant restaurant, good atmosphere, congenial company, quietly modulated conversation; then a waiter drops a plateful of food with a crash. The elderly lady looks up and slightly purses her lips in disapproval. The young man and woman have less control over their reactions and, mid-mouthful, drop their jaws in surprise. That describes it.

THE KILL

I concentrated here on tone and texture, trying in particular to show the colour similarities between the leopard's golden and black coat and the sunlight and shadow on the grass. Perfect camouflage. Although it might appear to be a laborious exercise, achieving this kind of grass texture does not take long. Laying the lighter tones sparingly with a fine brush onto a darker, mottled, still-wet base can produce the feeling of depth which I strive to obtain.

This leopard has killed a Grant's gazelle and hurriedly dragged it to deeper cover before other predators might attempt to steal it. Eventually, when it has caught its breath, the 90 lb leopard will carry its 120 lb prey high into the branches of a nearby tree.

slowly through the forest to the summit. It was like no other forest I have visited, strangely silent and brooding with the ancient, gnarled *Hagenia* trees somehow accentuating the feeling that this was Africa at its oldest. The memory of those few days will stay forever, a feeling not dissimilar to seeing those few mammoth tuskers in Ngorongoro crater.

My lung-searing scramble up Visoke was the ideal appetiser for the main event of the current safari, which was to climb Africa's highest peak, Mount Kilimanjaro, fulfilling an ambition thwarted nearly thirty years earlier by appendicitis. Here too, emotions were out of control. After the agony of the climb, the realisation that I was at the highest point of the continent, with a cloudless sky stretching to the horizon in all directions, was almost too much to take in.

Sandwiched between our memorable experiences among the extinct volcanoes of Rwanda and the heady triumph of conquering Kilimanjaro, we had witnessed the awesome spectacle of the wildebeest herds crossing the Mara River, camped on a wild and deserted island in Lake Victoria, walked through herds of buffalo, roan antelope, zebra and gazelles in the Western Serengeti, visited the fabled Ngorongoro Crater, and pitched our tent in the timeless baobab forests of Tarangire park with its great elephant herds. This was the ultimate safari encompassing some of the last untouched wonders of Africa.

It is indeed an ancient and mysterious land which has a profound effect on all but the most cynical. The visitors whom I have the privilege to introduce to the world of safari, in most cases, come from an affluent environment, perhaps having achieved their success by clawing and scratching their way up through the often sordid, so-called civilised world. They arrive worried about the state of affairs in their absence, bravely determined to enjoy the safari which they have mentally equated perhaps to China last year or Europe the year before – one more place to be ticked off on their check list of "recommended vacations".

ZEBRAS DRINKING

SAMBURU HERDSMAN

With our camel train we reached the foothills of the Ndoto Mountains in northern Kenya and camped the night beside a crystal clear stream. Before dawn the following morning, we climbed alone to explore the highlands and an hour later reached a small peak on top of which was an isolated Samburu *manyatta* (village). The inhabitants were astonished to see three white men, something some of the youngsters had never witnessed before. The cattle were just beginning to stir and a dog lay curled asleep in the cold dawn. An elder leant pensively on his spear, squinting into the rising sun as his eyes roved over his wealth. The scene was from a bygone, almost biblical, age.

Within days they are spellbound. At first it is the sheer profusion of animals but then, as time passes, I watch their faces and listen to their conversation and know that they have been hooked. This is no mere vacation, this is a deep experience of the soul.

Nobody has described the unsettling effect of African hypnosis more lucidly than the American adventurer, Negley Farson, who was strangely overwhelmed when he first witnessed bushmen dance their imitative Dance of the Kudu, in the Kalahari:

You were taken back until something unknown moved inside your soul; you were plagued by the feeling that stirred uneasily in your flesh and bones. Had you, on the long road to the You of today, ever danced like that?

This is not fantasy. It is an awareness as real for me, in Kenya, as it was for him in the Kalahari. I too have sensations of *déjà vu*, especially when I am alone on the sweeping plains of the Serengeti, or down in Olduvai Gorge, where early man once lived. It is as if this is not my first experience of Africa; that I have known these places somewhere in the past.

It is like coming home.

PUBLISHER'S ACKNOWLEDGEMENTS

The publishers are most grateful to The Greenwich Workshop, Dave Usher, Yvonne Goldsmith and Judy Davis, whose interest and assistance have been altogether invaluable in the preparation of this book. Also to Game Conservation International, Paula McGehee, who arranged for the photography of a number of paintings in the States; likewise to Nigel Pavitt for undertaking a similar exercise in Kenya.

We happened upon Simon's work by chance in Nairobi; largely thanks to Tony Duckworth, now of Funzi Island Fishing Camp near Shimoni. We are grateful to him for this, but more particularly for his wholehearted practical help from that time and for the marvellous hospitality extended to us, and to Simon and Susie, which has added considerably to the enjoyment of this venture. We might add that if the idea appeals of spending a few nights under canvas, surrounded by a hundred square miles of untouched bush and mangrove teeming with birdlife; together with the chance of a tarpon on fly, or a marlin … that's the place!

A number of people have helped us in various ways; to those who preferred not to be named, and to Ian Ballantine, Alan Binks, Jonah Belcher, Davis Brewer, Edward Bunting, Ben Carpenter, John and Shirley Chilton, Mike Fear, Aris Grammaticus, Peter Greenhalgh, Norman and Bridget Harrison, Betty Hawk, June Holloway, Jack and Pat Innes, Francine Leinhardt, Bill Longmuir, Peggy Mays, Fred Middleton, Nigel Partridge, Ian Philip, Desmond Reeves, Dick Roberts, Mike Scott, John and Nancy Schaeffer, Peter Shellard, Mike Sherrod, John Simpson, John Spurling, Stan Studer, Larry Sutcliffe, Edgar Turner, Vivien Ward and Vivien Williams we offer our sincere thanks.

Finally, we are grateful to Simon and Susie. Modest surprise and delight, respectively, gave way to graft when it became necessary; despite a tight painting schedule for a forthcoming exhibition in California. We are deeply indebted to Simon for his choice of priorities and, to both of them, for a lot of fun along the way.